WALKER
BOOKS

OOPS, I KIDNAPPED A PHARAOH!

LUAN GOLDIE

First published 2025 by Walker Books Ltd
87 Vauxhall Walk, London SE11 5HJ

2 4 6 8 10 9 7 5 3 1

Text © 2025 Luan Goldie
Cover and interior illustrations © 2025 Amy Nguyen

The right of Luan Goldie to be identified as author of
this work has been asserted in accordance with
the Copyright, Designs and Patents Act 1988

EU Authorized Representative: HackettFlynn Ltd, 36 Cloch Choirneal,
Balrothery, Co. Dublin, K32 C942, Ireland. EU@walkerpublishinggroup.com

This book has been typeset in ITC Berkeley Oldstyle

Printed and bound by CPI Group (UK) Ltd, Croydon CR0 4YY

British Library Cataloguing in Publication Data:
a catalogue record for this book is available from the British Library

ISBN 978-1-5295-1254-0

www.walker.co.uk

For Alexis,
The Yoongi to my Namjoon

1

LILAC-BLOODED

I sit on the bench outside of the school gates, perusing my AZ8 photocards and waiting for Dana to finish Jolly Geometry club. I know what you're thinking – what kind of weirdo would engage in an extracurricular maths activity on a Friday afternoon? And to that I would say: my spectacular bestie, of course.

My phone buzzes.

> Dana: OMG! This club is so fun.
> You should defo join next week.

I roll my eyes and giggle.

> Me: Hurry up and leave school. The
> greatest weekend of our lives is waiting!

I can't believe she has time for texting. We need to get started on our weekend of being superfans of the best band on the planet, AZ8. And as part of our celebrations, our double sleepover will consist of:

A Staying up both nights watching AZ8's finest music videos and eating junk.

B Two whole days at K-Mania, the world's biggest K-pop convention. It's a chance for us to stock up on merch such as photocards, T-shirts, posters and plushies, bubble tea beakers, plant pots, dishcloths and guitar picks. Personally, I've got my eye on the AZ8 wooden chopping board, because it's super cute *and* practical.

C Zero parental supervision.

Yeah, I said it.

Zero. Parental. Supervision.

My parents are away this weekend. Dad at one of the triathlons which seem to be increasingly taking over his life, and Mum at a textiles conference. Neither of them will be back until Sunday afternoon. That's nearly 50 hours of freedom with my bestie.

Of course, as I'm eleven, I'm not being left completely alone. No, Dana and I are being left in the care of the other *responsible* adult in my life: Nana. The same woman who once left six-year-old me at the brink of a waterfall while she went shopping for herbal medicines.

My phone rings. "Nana?" I answer. "So weird, I was just thinking about you."

"Skylar, I'm on my way to pick you up from school."

She's picking me up! Wow, that is unusually responsible of her. Maybe this time is going to be different...

"What school do you go to again?" she asks.

Or maybe not.

"Saint Margaret's Academy."

"I'm coming in a minute, right after I ask this gentleman where he bought his trilby," she says. "My dad used to wear a trilby, but his was blue and he won it in a raffle. I'll tell you about it when I see you." And she hangs up. Though I already know the story of my great-granddad's blue trilby hat and don't care to hear it again.

While waiting for Dana and Nana, I have a little scroll on K-popdontstop.com. Though there's nothing on AZ8 right now, because AZ8 are... Well, they're on a… Oh, it's still so difficult to talk about, but … AZ8 are on "a break".

Hashtag devastated.

They announced the news last month and, to be honest, Dana and I still haven't come to terms with it. I know they're not the first boy band in the world to take a break, and in the grand scheme of things it's not a big deal – boy bands take breaks to come back stronger; it's not because they're burnt out, hate each other or want to go solo – but I miss AZ8 with my *whole* heart!

Thank goodness for their seventeen albums, 25 tour videos, and over 200 hours of pre-recorded content that I can re-consume. I've also been extremely busy arranging my 1,276 AZ8 photocards. They are the most precious things I own. I would literally travel to the end of time for them.

I look behind me into the school yard. Still no sign of Dana.

I look up and down the road in front of school. Still no sign of Nana.

I pull up YouTube to pass the time. The home page has the video from new girl group Lilac Eyes in prime position.

Lilac Eyes. Pah! What a stupid name for a group.

Who cares that they're the hottest thing in K-pop right now, or that they're launching a range of limited-edition cat-shaped rucksacks, or that their lead dancer is afraid of the dark. I certainly don't.

The video for their single, "Water", was released four days ago and already has over fifteen million views. How did this happen? Sure, AZ8 videos get these types of views, but AZ8 have a loyal fanbase of billions. Lilac Eyes are fanless nobodies!

My curiosity gets the better of me, and I hit play.

Lilac Eyes begin an impeccable dance routine I can't help but admire – that spin! – and oooh, the vocals are stunning. And wow, the charisma of that visual is just— I hit pause and slam my phone down.

What am I doing? "Forgive me, AZ8," I cry, "for I have multi-stanned."

In K-pop, multi-stanning means being a stan, or fan, of more than one group, and not only is it looked down upon, it's also exhausting trying to keep up with multiple bands.

Anyway, it's not like I'm going to become a Lilac Eyes fan, or Lilac Teer as they're called. I'm an AZ8 Glow for ever. Though, hmm, it is important to know your enemies. I flip my phone over and let it play to the super well-written English chorus.

Water runs through your fingers, ooh I make it linger, tinga tinga tinga.

I tap my foot. It's so infectious and—

A horn blasts and a cloud of smoke billows up around me. I waft away the fumes to reveal Nana's electric three-wheeled minivan, which she bought last month to help grow her food truck business. The tuk-tuk is emerald green, with a swirl of pink writing on the side which says *Purrito's Burritos.*

"Hi, Nana. You know, you didn't have to pick me up; I usually get the bus."

Nana scratches at her hair under her big orange headwrap and squints at something on her phone.

"Is everything OK?" I ask.

She hops down from the tuk-tuk and wipes her permanently greasy hands along the front of her rhinestone-covered jeans. "Cha-ching!" she cries. "I just received a huge order for a very specific type of sweet burrito."

"Sweet burrito?" I turn my nose up. "Gross."

The tuk-tuk's motor backfires with a loud blast and I jump. "Why did it do that? No one's even sitting in the driver's seat."

"I think it's something to do with the moon," she says with a wave of her hand. "Skylar" – she fixes her gaze on mine – "have I ever told you how beautiful the full moon used to look back when I was a child? Especially on Tuesdays…"

"Yes, Nana. Several times." I don't mean to be rude, but Nana's stories from childhood are long and confusing and there's not a single one I haven't heard a hundred times already.

"I'll tell you more on the way to the market," she says. "Get in."

"Hang on, we're waiting for Dana. She's staying over this weekend. Remember?"

A deep line forms between Nana's brows. "Which one is Dana?"

I huff. "Dana is my bestie in the whole wide world."

Nana snaps her fingers, "Ah yes, that little boy with the moustache?"

"Er, no. Dana's the…" I check back into the school yard and spot her lingering. "There she is. Let me go get her."

I can't believe I'm walking *back* into school. "Dana!" I yell, but she doesn't hear me. I try several more times as I cross the yard towards her. She's standing with a group of kids I don't know, all of them wearing headphones. As I get closer, I realize they're all doing a strange little dance, which involves swaying their hips side to side in a liquid-like manner.

I have the distinct feeling of being left out.

"Dana," I try, "what are you doing?" But she can't hear me over whatever she's listening to. "Dana?"

Nothing.

Maybe it's frustration because I've been waiting for so long, or maybe it's that I really don't like this left out feeling, but something propels me to pull off her neon-green cat-ear headphones.

"Skylar!" she yells in shock. "Oh no!"

Then I hear it: the unmistakable sound of a thumping beat, bumping baseline and catchy lyrics of *tinga tinga tinga!* coming from her headphones.

"You're listening to Lilac Eyes?" I cry. "How could you? We're Glows. That means we only ever listen to AZ8's music."

Dana's face goes into panic mode – the same look she gets when she thinks she's left the lights on in a room somewhere.

"Skylar, it's not what you think!"

"Really? It sounds pretty clear to me," I say, indicating her headphones. The sound of "Water" plays between us, the lead crooner's silky soft voice the soundtrack to this most devastating moment.

Dana shakily tries to switch it off, but wrongly turns it up before finally the music ceases. "I can explain," she starts.

"Don't bother. It's clearer than Haru's skin after a week of not eating deep-fried food what's going on here. You're a—"

She shakes her head and pleads, "No, don't say it."

"You're a … you're a…" She's a multi-stan – that's it, that's what I'm going to call her. A multi-stan. A traitor. A defector.

"You're right." Dana drops her head, and her long red straggly hair falls in front of her face. "I'm a Lilac Teer," she mumbles guiltily.

I can't believe it! How could she do this to AZ8? To me? I turn on my heel and stomp back across the school yard.

"Wait!" Dana calls as she runs after me. "Skylar, slow down."

I turn back to point an accusatory finger. "You entered a deal, Dana. You said you would love AZ8 for ever, for richer or poorer, in sickness and health, through beautiful hairstyles and totally misguided hairstyles, till death do you part."

"I know and I do, but … but…" She stops. "I still like AZ8."

"Like?" I holler. "*Like* is a way to describe your feelings for a particular pasta shape or bus route or family member. Not for describing your feelings for a group of eight life-changing geniuses."

Dana takes a shaky breath. "I'm just ready to stan someone else for a bit, especially while AZ8 are broken up."

"They're not broken up," I snap. "They're having a break."

The horn beeps and I storm towards Nana. I'm fuming. I just want to go home, put on my favourite AZ8 sad songs playlist and think about the death of my friendship.

Something brushes my back and I whip around to see Dana trailing behind. "What are you doing? Stop following me."

"We're having a sleepover, remember?"

"Why would we still do that?" I ask.

"Quickly, girls!" Nana shouts over the weird whining noise of the engine. "I've got to pick up the shopping."

I chuck my rucksack and photobook on the back seat, then pause to look at Dana. She swishes her mouth side to side, then says quietly, "I was really excited about hanging out with you this weekend. About sleeping over and going to K-Mania."

I don't know what to do. Deep down I *do* still want her to stay over, but I'm also angry. She's betrayed the very thing that made us friends in the first place.

"How can we be friends after what you said about AZ8?" I ask.

"Because we have more in common than AZ8, and we— Ow! Why are you pushing us?"

Nana has jumped down from the tuk-tuk and is hustling us both into the back seat. "You girls must think I have all day," she complains.

Before we've even done up our seat belts, Nana's in the front and revving the engine. "We have to be fast; the tuk-tuk will need its rest soon. Plus, I have two kilos of onions at home and they aren't going to peel themselves."

The tuk-tuk sets off and the radio comes on, just as an announcer says, "For all you Korean pop music fans out there, here's the debut song from new girl group sensation, Lilac Eyes. The group will be in London this weekend to perform their hit single, "Water", at K-Mania."

Dana gasps, then begins to sway.

I get my phone and play AZ8's "My Heart Goes Dry When You Stop Loving Me" to combat the sound of Lilac Eyes.

Dana leans forward and calls to Nana, "Could you turn it up, please?"

"Sure," Nana says. "Tuk-tuk, please turn up volume."

The vehicle fills with the sound of *those girls* singing. I cross my arms, furious.

Our heads whip to the left as the tuk-tuk takes a tight corner, narrowly missing a Food2Go driver on an electric scooter. This is really fast.

"Nana!" I wail over the clashing sounds of *my* music (which is excellent), Lilac Eyes on the radio (which is grating, yet a little catchy), and the spluttering engine of the tuk-tuk. "Could you please slow down?"

"Yeah," Dana agrees as she rubs her tummy. "I had three helpings of minty mushy peas at lunch and, as much as I enjoyed them, I don't need to see them again."

I roll my eyes. "What kind of person would eat mushy peas by choice? Especially when sugar snap peas, the greatest of all the peas, exist."

"The kind of person who values British cuisine," Dana fires back.

I grip my photobook with all my might as the tuk-tuk doesn't slow down, as requested, but speeds up.

"Nana," I try again. "Why are you in such a rush?"

"Because I need to do my shopping!" she yells. "When it comes to burritos, people want something new. They want exciting, they want tasty, they want sweet." She gestures wildly and the tuk-tuk sways left to right. "And I know just the place to find the sweetest wild figs in the world."

"Tesco?" I cry out in panic, now gripping the edge of my seat.

Nana laughs. "Tuk-tuk," she yells, "Tuk-tuk, take me to the place in my mind's eye."

Her mind's eye. What does that mean?

The tuk-tuk takes yet another sharp corner – who knew the city was so angular? – and I fly into Dana's side. She links her arm with mine and we brace ourselves as sparks fly up the side of the vehicle. Yellow lights flash and … is that the smell of burning rubber?

"Nana, slow down! This is dangerous driving."

"When the smart speaker works, all you need is speed!" Nana shouts. "Speed is how we get there."

"Get *where*?" I call.

"To the place in my mind's eye." She removes her hands from the steering wheel and places them over her eyes.

What is she doing?! With no driver and some very vague instructions, the tuk-tuk propels us towards a huge glowing white oval that has suddenly appeared right ahead of us.

"What's going on?" Dana asks as she grips my arm tightly.

"I'm not sure," I reply, as I tuck my photobook under the seat belt for extra safety, "but I don't like it."

The oval flashes purple, green and turquoise, and begins to flicker around the outside edges. It's stunning and terrifying at the same time and now … now, we're lifting off the ground and heading right for it…

"Girls," Nana shouts, "hold on!"

The oval glares impossibly bright. I close my eyes and hold onto Dana as though my life depends on it as we fly right into the terrifying glowing circle in the sky.

2

SAND, SAND EVERYWHERE AND NOT A DROP TO DRINK

I blink my eyes open and check I'm still in one piece. Then I check my AZ8 photobook is still safely tucked under the seat belt. Finally, I check Dana, who is clutching onto me tightly and frowning. "Are those palm trees?" she asks.

I follow her gaze out of the tuk-tuk. We're surrounded by the long feather-like leaves of palm trees. Interesting…

Nana turns to face us. I wouldn't quite say her expression is one of guilt, but it's definitely not a picture of innocence. "Now, girls, I'm going to need you to do a tiny favour for me."

Nana's favours are never good, and usually involve me being her kitchen assistant and having to peel an entire box of seasoning cubes or grate beetroots till my hands turn purple.

"A teeny-weeny, tiny favour," she adds.

"It depends on what it is," I reply hesitantly.

"I need you both to wait here for me, silently, unquestioningly and unmovingly."

"Unmovingly is not a real word," Dana says.

"Yes, it is. I'm an adult; I know all the words." Nana laughs and reaches into her pocket, then pulls out a fan of ten-pound notes. "I'm also an adult who made a ton of moolah delivering kebab-style burritos to office workers this week." She raises an eyebrow. "Would either of you like extra cashish to spend on sequins and glitter at your P-Rock event this weekend?"

"She's trying to bribe us," Dana whispers.

"I know," I whisper back. "Isn't it great?"

Nana wafts the money back and forth creating a very welcome breeze, because all of a sudden, it's freakishly warm.

"We're happy to accept your offer." I reach forward to grab a note. "We won't move, but can you at least explain what's going on? You said we were going shopping but—"

Nana's headwrap jiggles as she shakes her head at us. "No, no, no. Remember, *unquestioningly*. Dinkie deal?" She sticks out her two pinkies.

"Pinkie promise," I correct.

"I need ten minutes," Nana says. "Then we'll go home and I'll cook you both anything you want." She wiggles her pinkies. "English food? Scottish food? Welsh or Northern Irish food?"

I turn my nose up at the suggested cuisines.

"Korean food?" Nana tries.

I clap. "Now we're talking. Your beef bulgogi is banging."

I join pinkies with Nana's and we both look to Dana. "Hold on a precious minute," she says. "You really expect us not to ask any questions?"

Nana bites her bottom lip, then shoves two ten-pound notes Dana's way.

I nudge Dana in the side and, with a sigh, she exchanges the money for her pinkie.

"You're good girls." Nana smiles, raises her arms to push away some of the palm leaves, then disappears.

I sit back in my seat, confused. Very, very confused.

Dana pouts. "So," she says, "we're going to sit here and wait."

"Yup," I agree. "We're 100 per cent not going to check out where we are or what's going on."

"Nu-uh," Dana says as she looks at her money. "Not at all. I'm not even a miniscule bit curious."

"Me neither."

"I literally don't care what happened, why we drove into a giant oval of light or why it's forty degrees."

I agree. "And I don't even care that we're surrounded by date palm trees, which only really thrive in hot dry climates."

Dana wide-eyes me. "How do you know that?"

"Because I watch a lot of gardening shows with my dad. Well, at least I used to." Ever since Dad started training for triathlons, he falls asleep on the sofa before "Gardeners' World" even begins. I try to remember the last time we did something together without him falling asleep or rushing off for some kind of training.

Dana and I sit in silence until I decide I can't take any more and part the leaves like curtains.

"WHOA!" I exclaim.

No wonder the heat is so intense – we're in the middle of a desert. All I can see for miles are rolling yellow sand dunes and bright blue skies.

We both step out of the tuk-tuk onto grainy, yellow softness. I grab a handful then watch as it slinks through my fingers. Usually, I find playing with sand super relaxing, but there's something about this situation which makes me feel a little on edge. Maybe it's the fact that one moment we were on the high street and the next we were...

"Where are we?" I ask.

"I don't know, but, whoa' ... sand," Dana observes, rather unhelpfully, because sand is the one thing I've already managed to establish.

"Where in the world has this much sand?" I wonder, then I gasp. "Maybe we're in Dubai. Ooh, I've always wanted to go to that hotel with the giant fish tank and gold-plated hamburgers."

Dana narrows her eyes. "This isn't glitzy enough to be Dubai. It could be the Sahara Desert?"

"How cool," I say. "So, I'm thinking camel ride, followed by sandboarding, followed by a pit barbecue under the stars and— Why are you furrowing your brow like that?"

Dana spreads her arms. "Do you see any other tourists?"

It really is quite vast out here, and apart from a few scurrying scarab beetles by our feet, there's not a smidgen of life in sight. "On second thoughts," I say, "maybe we should just sit here *unmovingly* and wait for Nana."

Dana nods. "I don't want us to get lost."

We both flop onto the sand with our backs to the tuk-tuk and talk over what happened. The speeding. The glowing oval. Nana looking excited and … what was it she said? Something about sweet wild figs and going to "the place in my mind's eye". It makes no sense.

I mop my moist brow. "The desert is such a nice setting," I say. "No wonder AZ8 filmed five music videos in deserts. Do you remember that amazing dance routine in the video for 'Beauty is the Beast I Love'? It was legendary."

Dana huffs. "I have no idea how they didn't faint wearing all that leather."

I bounce my shoulders and sing, "*If you love my face, my beauty, then you love the beast. From my hair to my feet, I'm a beautiful treat.*" Then in an effort to mimic Haru in the stunning music video, which rightly won five ABCDGVP Awards, I jump up and attempt a triple pirouette. However, my feet get stuck, and I topple over. "Doh! Rotating in sand is not easy."

Despite the sweat rolling off her head, Dana gives it a go too and falls even faster. "Impossible."

"Not for AZ8," I say, "but then, they defy logic."

"No, they don't." She laughs. "The whole point of logic is that it's correct reasoning."

I wipe my neck on the polyester of my school tie. "I can't believe their make-up didn't sweat off when they danced in the desert. Incredible. Do you ever just sit and think about how amazing AZ8 are?"

"How amazing AZ8 *were*," Dana says. "AZ8 are past tense, Skylar."

I feel my face redden – not just from the unacceptable temperature, but from anger at how Dana is using grammar to talk down AZ8. I cross my legs and try to distract myself from the harsh realities of life by pouring sand from one hand to another.

"I'm sorry," Dana says. "Dehydration makes me mean. I'd literally do anything for a kiwi kombucha right now."

I reach into the tuk-tuk for my rucksack and pull out the bottle I was saving for after school. "It's a little warm, but we can share."

Dana smiles gratefully and we pass the bottle between us.

"How long has Nana been gone now?" I ask.

Dana checks her watch and frowns. "Urgh, it's dead. But judging from my rate of sunburn, I'd say she's well over ten minutes, which means she's broken the pinkie promise."

"Let's go find her."

We help each other up, chuck our school blazers in the tuk-tuk, and exit the gathering of trees.

"I don't understand how we travelled so far," I say.

"Me neither. It's like the speed of the tuk-tuk opened up some kind of space-travelling transportation system."

"Space travel?" I squawk. "This definitely isn't space."

"No," Dana chuckles. "I didn't mean literal space as in molecular hydrogen, dark matter and little green aliens; I meant more like how time travel dilation can happen in line with space travel."

I stop to remove my tie, because overheating is not helping me follow Dana's train of thought. "I don't think we've time travelled either, because if we had it would be obvious – there would be dinosaurs or…"

"Knights in shining armour," Dana offers as she also removes her tie.

"Or there would be wooden houses." I duck down to roll off my tights.

"Or horses and carriages," Dana adds as she discards her tights as well.

"People looking at us strangely like, *Wooo, are those two girls from the future?*" I say while slipping my shoes back on. "Yuck, I have sand between my toes."

"Me too," Dana cringes, just as a loud braying noise

causes us to jump. Appearing from behind the cluster of trees is a super cute donkey accompanied by a man wearing a white sheet around his waist.

"Eee-aww!" the donkey says.

"Hello, kind sir," I say to the man. "We're a little lost. Have you perhaps seen a small woman, about this high, last seen wearing a sparkling pair of rhinestone jeans and an orange headwrap. Smells of fried onions, garlic and smoked paprika."

The man stares at us blankly.

"Try something else," Dana murmurs.

I huff. I really am getting hot and bothered here.

"Do you know where we can get an ice cream?" I ask.

The man raises a finger and points behind us, beyond the trees. *Ahhh*, we never thought to look there. I take Dana's hand and together we pass the trees.

"Whoa!" we say in unison as a grand structure comes into view.

"A hotel," I reason uncertainly. "Of course."

"Yes, a hotel," Dana replies in an equally unsure voice. "A normal, modern-day hotel. Nothing strange about that."

We stumble across the sand in silence towards the cluster of grand buildings surrounded by columns decorated with colourful patterns and symbols. It isn't until we stop at the entrance and look up at the two giant and pristine sphinx statues that we dare confront the horrible truth. One, there's probably nowhere to get a gold-plated hamburger around here, and two, we've possibly time travelled.

3

YOUNG RULER

"Ancient Egypt!" Dana squeals for the 50th time this minute. "Just how ... *how* did this happen?" She laughs hysterically as we pass under a huge arch into the grounds of what looks much more like a palace than a hotel. "Time travel is impossible. The greatest minds of the world couldn't make it happen, yet – and no offence to your nana – she's somehow cracked it."

"Nana *is* pretty clever," I say. "At home, when the Internet stops working, it's Nana who fixes it."

"Still. Time travel?" Dana flings her head back and laughs, the sound echoing around the vast courtyard we've stepped into. She walks over to a monumental sculpture of a man in a skirt and hugs its feet. "This is the most thrilling day of my life."

We're gathering stares from onlookers. "Shh," I try as I pull her away from the sculpture. "You're getting carried away. It's probably not" – I lean closer to whisper in her ear – "time travel. We'll ask Nana when we find her. *If* we find her."

"Of course we'll find her, because, plot spoiler, she isn't going to blend in."

Dana's right and we definitely don't fit in here either.

To our left there's a huge marketplace, crammed with bustling, busy, shouting people. The men wear tiny white sheets around their waists while the women are in long dresses. Each of them has a different hairstyle, from wavy curls to fancy plaits decorated with flowers and beads. There's also a gorgeous smell of heavy rich perfume. To our right there's a craft area, filled with people sitting on rugs sewing, painting and sculpting pots. There's so much going on, I feel slightly overwhelmed.

Dana claps her hands. "It's incredible. We're not only *literally* history, we're also about to *go down* in history for being part of your nana's scientifically momentous voyage."

Excited cries draw us towards a large gathering ahead. "Do you think all these people are staring at Nana?" I ask as we move through the crowd, trying to get a closer look.

"I don't know, but this is giving me strong ancient Egyptian public entertainment vibes."

"Ohmygosh, what does that mean?" I panic.

"Is someone going to get mauled by a lion? Or put in a pillory and splatted with rotten fruit?"

We finally push to the front where a large courtyard is set up for some kind of show. A group of people in blue robes carrying goblet drums appear and sit on the ground facing the crowd. They begin to pat out a simple beat. It's pretty good actually and I can't help but tap along. They're joined by a flute player and a harpist who really amp things up. Whoa, these ancient folks have some jams.

"Stop dancing," Dana says. "You're going to draw too much attention to us. Don't you know how to keep a low profile?"

"Yes, like AZ8 when they're moving through an international airport," I say. "Face masks, sunglasses and *no autographs please*."

Dana chuckles as I do my best impression of Yujun trying to bat away photographers.

Then, from behind a flowing curtain, a boy around our age emerges, and the crowd goes wild, clapping and cheering. He's wearing a floor-length shimmering gold cape and leans slightly to one side on a gold cane. As he steps closer, drinking in the audience's applause, I notice that the cane's handle is shaped as a lizard head. Very cool.

Suddenly, the boy throws his arms in the air, causing his cape to billow up around him. The beat drops and he sashays across the floor.

"Who. Is. That?" Dana asks.

"I have no idea," I say, "but he is super impressive, and his eyeliner game is strong."

We watch as the boy spins, dips and crunches in time with the music. As he twirls towards us, I get a good close look at him and can't help but think he looks so very, very familiar...

More dancers slide in from all different directions and launch into a slick, highly synchronized routine, which involves lots of body popping and circling on the floor. They reach into their robes and pull out handfuls of coloured sand, which they throw into the air, creating a path of raining sand for the boy to run through.

"Whoa!" I applaud wildly.

Dana starts snapping her fingers, which she only does when something is extra impressive. "I had no idea ancient civilizations had such strong production values when it came to entertainment. Also, I think I'm his biggest fan."

"I thought you were too busy being in love with Lilac Eyes to appreciate *real* talent anymore."

Dana peels her eyes from the boy for one moment to narrow them at me. "Whatever," she replies.

The boy shimmies over to us and slams his cane on the ground, before twirling around it. My heart beats fast and I can feel my adrenalin spiking. I'm finding it really hard not to join in, because this type of joyful dancing is contagious. "This is sensational," I say as the ancient Egyptian groove infects me.

Dana grabs my wrist. "Don't do it, Skylar."

I growl at the effort of not being allowed to dance. Oh, how I want to hop on this dance floor and spin around in sand right now. Gosh, I want it more than anything – except of course finding Nana, going home to some beef bulgogi, and news of an immediate AZ8 reunion. I settle for stepping one pointy toe, then another, onto the boy's dance floor. Then, a little one, two step, a tiny burst of Gangnam galloping and—

"Stop it," Dana says. "We can't draw attention to ourselves."

"I know, it's just … hang on." I split from the crowd to do a quick boogie.

I get the gist of the boy's routine quite quickly and really sass it up. The crowd are loving me and chant to encourage my moves. The boy, however, doesn't appear pleased to be sharing the attention and immediately tries to outdance me. When I do some fancy floorwork, he does a head spin; when I shimmy, he shakes like a snake; and when I do a high kick, he drops into a squat with his arms folded as his legs shoot out in the greatest Ukrainian hopak I've ever seen.

I bust out some of my special K-pop moves and the crowd goes crazy. The boy dances closer and I raise my hand for a high five, but instead he nudges me so hard I fall back into Dana's arms. How rude!

The boy glides back to the centre, where he butterflies his legs and finishes with a dab. The whole audience erupts into applause as he takes a bow.

Dana quirks an eyebrow. "Why does he look familiar?"

"I was thinking the exact same thing, like I know him, though I don't actually know him." This is so strange, I think, as I watch the boy take two more bows.

"It's like I've seen him, but not actually seen him," Dana explains.

I nod. "It's like I've heard about him, but not actually heard about him."

Hmm. We stare at the little superstar as he takes another bow – seriously, this is his fifth: he's really milking it. The crowd love it, though; they rapturously cheer and then start to chant, "Tut! Tut! Tut!"

"Tut?" I repeat. "Cool name."

"It is," Dana agrees. "Tut. Short. Snappy. Unusual."

"Tut," I say again, as if testing the word on my lips. "Tut. Could it be short for something? Tutsan?"

"Or Tutyan," Dana suggests.

"Perhaps even Tutbam," I offer.

Then someone in the crowd yells, *"All hail! Tutankhamun."*

What? I rub my ears as if sensing they're filled with nonsense. Then, again, the call of, *"All hail, Tutankhamun."*

Excuse me, but what?!

Dana slaps her own cheeks and says, "Oh my Michelle Obama! Is that the boy king, the legendary Tutankhamun? Yes, it must be. That means we're—"

"In ancient Egypt," I say. "Yes. We established that already."

"Ancient Egypt spanned 3,000 years."

I smile because I am, as always, endlessly impressed with how much knowledge is stacked inside my best friend's cute little head. "Is that really him, though?"

Dana studies the boy as he runs around getting high fives from the crowd. "He looks about ten or eleven, so I'd say we're in 1331BC."

"Pfft," I laugh. "It's all ancient to me."

"I can't believe that actual Tutankhamun is here. Do you think he'd be up for a selfie?"

"Great idea! Should we try and get close?"

We survey the increasingly rowdy mass of fans around Tut then, just as we're about to make our way over, Tut shouts something and makes a break for it.

"Where's he going?" I ask, delighted by the spectacle of the boy king taking off through the palace grounds.

"There's no way he's going to outrun that many people," Dana comments.

But he somehow manages to sprint away, ducking and diving anytime someone gets close. At one point it appears as if Tut is heading straight for us, but in a flash of gold and eyeliner, he cuts away and disappears into the marketplace, leaving his fan boys and fan girls bewildered.

"So much for getting a selfie," I say, impressed by Tut's disappearing act.

"Skylar," Dana yells suddenly, "your nana is over there!"

"Where?"

Dana grabs me by the face and points it in the right direction. "Over there, in the market area, by those stalls."

Nana fills a wicker basket with produce and laughs

with a stallholder. I must say, she looks exceptionally carefree for someone who was on the school run and ended up time travelling with two minors in her care.

"Nana!" I shout as we run towards her.

"Skylar. Dana." She stomps over. "I told you two not to move. What happened to dinkie deal?"

"Pinkie promise," I correct … again. "And yes, we tried but, Nana, you need to tell us what's going on. Why have we…" I drop my voice. "Why have we time travelled?"

Nana ignores the question and hands each of us a papyrus poster of Tut standing in front of a gleaming sun.

"This is cute," Dana giggles, as she gazes at her poster.

"Nana, you said ten minutes, but you were waaay longer."

She wriggles her headwrap, making it sit lopsidedly. "Not my fault, the lines at the merch stands were crazy long. And you know what's strange?" she says over her shoulder as she walks off.

Dana and I totter behind. "Er, yeah," I call, trying to catch up. "Everything."

"They didn't sell keyrings," Nana huffs. "I once had a keyring shaped as a capybara. I got it from the zoo when I was—"

"Tell me everything!" Dana interrupts excitedly.

"About capybaras?" Nana asks.

Dana grabs Nana by the arm. "No, about time travel. How did you do it? Did you discover a wormhole? Is it to do with travelling faster than the speed of light? Have you reported your discovery to CERN?"

"And more importantly," I jump in, "where do we think Tut got his outfit from, because I could totally rock a gold skirt?"

Dana tuts impatiently. "How does it work? Can you go back to any point in time? Does it go forward too? Does it—"

"Gah! Too many questions." Nana stops to switch her wicker basket from one arm to another. "I don't have answers, but I do have an order for seventy sweet'n'wild fig and falafel burritos I need to get made."

Dana chokes out a laugh. "You're telling me you time travelled to buy figs? No way. Is this something you do often?"

Nana shrugs and says in an unnaturally high voice, "Of course not, it was an accident. This has *never* happened before."

We obediently follow Nana out of the palace grounds and back towards the gathering of trees, all while pelting her with questions she doesn't answer.

"Get in," she orders as we reach the tuk-tuk.

We both jump in the back and watch as Nana hits the big red button, then says to the smart speaker, "Tuk-tuk, take me to the place in my mind's eye."

I grasp hold of Dana and we both scream as the portal opens and the tuk-tuk zooms in.

4

SLEEPOVER

I'm gasping for breath as we land outside my house. I jump out of the tuk-tuk and kneel as if to kiss the ground, because it feels suitably dramatic, but once my mouth is inches away from it, I come to my senses and – yuck!

"What are you doing?" Dana cries as she waves billowing smoke away from her face. "Don't you know how many germs and microbes live on the average metropolitan pavement?"

"I got carried away," I say as I right myself. "I'm just so happy to be in the present day again. Phew."

"Yes, phew indeed," Dana says as she hands me my rucksack and photobook. "That ride home was really something."

Now we both look to Nana who is coughing in the smoke. She leans forward to tap a flashing blue light on the dashboard. "The tuk-tuk's tired," she says. "It won't be able to make another trip today."

"I'm pleased to hear that," Dana says. "Because as much as time travel is incredible, the dangers associated with it are huge. One wrong move and we could have wiped out the whole of humanity. I feel we should put this significant scientific breakthrough on ice, at least until I can write up a thorough risk assessment."

"Dangers?" I laugh. "What dangers? There's nothing dangerous about Nana."

"I'm talking about the butterfly effect," Dana says plainly.

"You really need to get over your irrational fear of butterflies."

It makes no sense that Dana loves the natural world like I love Yujun in a cosy heavy knit jumper, yet she's terrified of butterflies.

Nana frowns. "Why would anyone be scared of butterflies?"

"Because," Dana says in a loud voice, "they're creepy and flappy and show-offy."

"Where I grew up there were thousands of butterflies." Nana makes a fluttering wing motion with her hands. "Big, gorgeous orange ones."

Dana shudders. "Please can we talk about something else? Like, what powers this thing anyway?"

"Waste," Nana says flatly.

"Are we talking poop here?" I ask, slightly grossed out.

"No, silly. Food waste. Vegetable peelings, eggshells, those crusty end bits of bread nobody likes."

I love the crusty ends of bread and had been wondering where they'd been going.

"I don't know why it keeps billowing smoke," Nana murmurs. "I must ask Akua about it."

"Who's Akua?" I enquire.

"Akua, from the dental surgery," Nana answers cryptically. "It's funny, because when I was a baby, I had a pet rabbit called Akua. She only had one ear and…"

While this roving and completely irrelevant story plays out, Dana makes her way around the back of the tuk-tuk, pops open the boot and screams.

Nana and I both run to her. I'm half expecting to see a parking ticket or an infestation of ancient Egyptian scarab beetles, but instead a pile of burrito wrappers falls away to reveal a small boy in a gold outfit and fabulous eyeliner.

"Tutankhamun?" I gasp.

He flicks his big eyes back and forth between us, then grins.

Nana's mouth drops open, and Dana slaps herself on the forehead.

"Tutankhamun?" I say again, in the hope someone will respond because I feel there's a possibility this is not real at all.

Tutankhamun stands to his full height, which isn't very much, and leans on my head as he steps out of the boot.

"Ouch!' I yell.

He slams shut the boot and climbs on top of the tuk-tuk. He raises his cane in the air and shrieks, "Heee heee!" Then he does a high kick and hip thrust before shouting, "OOOOO!" into the sky.

"Hmm," I say, "this doesn't feel like something we should be allowing to happen."

"I know," Dana agrees, "but his charisma is really scene stealing."

"TU-TAN-KHA-MUN!" he yells, followed by a long string of other words I don't understand. People are beginning to come to their windows and stare. I grab at him. "Get down," I try. "Why are you so loud?"

"Wooo!" Tut shrieks as he finally slips off the boot. He laughs as we jostle him away from the tuk-tuk and into the house before any of my nosy neighbours get too curious. Once inside, he takes off his sandals and proceeds to throw them at the wall one by one before strutting to the living room where he snaps his fingers at my cat, Kookie.

"Oh, she doesn't like strangers," I warn. But Kookie literally leaps into Tut's open arms. That furry little traitor – she's never done that to me before.

Tut sits down on the sofa, with Kookie cradled in his arms.

"What now?" I ask.

"I don't know," Dana says. "I guess we keep him safe till your nana fixes the tuk-tuk and we can return him to his rightful place in history. It's cool watching him, though, like a documentary come to life."

Tut gets up from the sofa, walks over to my dad's towering cheese plant – his pride and joy – and snaps off the biggest leaf.

I gasp in utter horror. "My dad's going to burst a blood vessel."

Tut hands the leaf to Dana and instructs her to fan him with it. And always a sucker for a direct instruction, she does! She actually fans King Tut with a previously thriving Monstera Deliciosa leaf, like it's a palm frond and she's a servant.

I try to appeal to her common sense. "Dana, what on earth are you doing? He looks about ten years old. You're not meant to be his personal air conditioner."

"I don't want him to overheat," she says, her face reddening with exertion.

Tut lies down, taking up the whole sofa. He wriggles his sandy toes, then lets out a soft sigh of relaxation.

We hear the front door open and a few seconds later Nana bounds into the living room. "There's a little problem, a teeny-weeny, tiny one." Nana holds her thumb and forefinger to illustrate the size of the problem, which I'm going to guess is exceptionally underestimated. But before she can explain, her belly lets out the most enormous rumble. "First, food." And with that, she walks back out.

Dana and I listen to the sounds of the fridge, the microwave, then plates, before Nana re-enters the living room balancing multiple plates on her arms. "Dinner time," she announces as if everything is normal.

I'm getting quite wound up. "This is no time for cuisine. Tell us if the tuk-tuk is working again?"

"Please say yes," Dana begs. "Because me becoming a slave was not on my bingo card for this weekend."

Tut chuckles and booms the word "Slave" while pointing at Dana.

"No!" she cries, seriously offended. "I'm a friend. Can you say *friend*?"

Nana interrupts the language lesson with the suggestion of, "Feta cheese, olive and pepper burrito?"

"Feta cheese?" I say, caught between the growl in my stomach and the ever-increasing anxiety about Tut being here.

"Yes," Nana says. "And Skylar, I added extra balsamic vinegar to give it that zing you like so much."

"It's true," I say defeatedly, my hunger winning. "I do love food with zing." I take a plate and – whoa! – I never thought I could love a microwaved salad-based snack this much.

I help Dana, who is still busy fanning Tut, to take a bite of her own burrito. "Yummy," she says. "It's like summer on a Greek island, without the environment-destroying air miles."

"Mmm," I agree, marvelling at the salty, balsamic goodness. But … no! Hang on! "Nana, stop trying to distract us with delicious food."

"Yeah, Nana," Dana mouths as balsamic vinegar drips down her chin. "What are we doing about the whole problem of having a boy king from 1331BC in our possession?"

At this, Tut flicks open his eyes, gestures to Dana's plate and opens his mouth.

"Now he wants you to *feed* him?" I say, almost in disgust. I take half of my burrito and shove it into his waiting mouth.

"The tuk-tuk is having some issues," Nana announces.

I scoff. "You can say that again."

"The tuk-tuk is having some issues," she repeats. "I, of course, don't know why it decided to time travel. What a strange, unexpected and never-happened-before incident." Her eyes dart everywhere around the room apart from me.

"Nana," I say quite seriously, "are you telling us the truth?"

"Yes," she says while fiddling with her headwrap. "A little old woman like me would never lie. Anyway, I spoke to Akua from the dental surgery, and she said the tuk-tuk needs a good night's rest and refuelling. It also needs a new Flux-FSCH-88 to stop all the smoke."

I panic. "Do we have a Flux-FSCH-88?"

"No, I ordered one from dodgyparts.com, but even with express delivery it won't arrive until tomorrow lunchtime, which means Tut will have to spend the night."

"What?" I shout.

Tut makes a noise which sounds like "Hmm ymm ymm" and indicates for more food.

"Here," Nana says, as she takes the rest of *my* burrito and hands it to him. "He's a fabulous eater, isn't he? Maybe we should keep him."

"No," Dana protests. "We can't go around history stealing royalty because we like the way they enjoy Mediterranean-inspired burritos."

"No," I agree. "And I don't like the way my cat has fallen in love with him."

At this, Kookie stands up to stretch, pads in a circle, and lies back down on Tut's belly.

"Feta cheese," Tut says and points to his mouth.

"Good boy," Nana says, giving him a thumbs up. "And you're right, it is feta cheese. Now, kids, we have a long day ahead of us tomorrow, what with taking this one home and your K-Popcorn Mania."

"K-Mania!" Dana says in shock. "With everything that's happened over the last few hours I almost forgot it's tomorrow."

"Me too." I narrow my eyes at her. "I also *almost* forgot that you're a Lilac Teer."

Dana pouts. "I can't believe you still want to have a fan war with me. Aren't there bigger things to concentrate on right now?"

I look around at the most peculiar of Friday night living room scenes and yes, she's right. I don't have the energy to waste on people who choose to stan lesser groups. I need my energy for more important things in life, like sorting out this disaster and getting that limited-edition AZ8 wooden chopping board.

"I just remembered something," Nana squeals.

"What?" Dana and I ask hopefully, anticipating a tuk-tuk solution.

"I need to take the chicken out of the freezer for tomorrow's dinner."

We put Tut in my big brother's room. Jesse is away at a music festival this weekend, so it should be fine. What's not fine is the fact that Kookie climbs into his bed too. Kookie, who has slept on my bed every night since we got her.

"Goodnight, Tut," we say.

"Goodnight, slave," he replies with a yawn.

"Friend," Dana says, pointing at herself, but it's too late: Tut's eyes are already closing and within seconds he's asleep.

We gently close the door, then tiptoe into my room, where I unroll Dana my special-edition AZ8 sleeping bag from their one-time seminal reality show *AZ8 in the Alps*. Dana smiles as she strokes it. "Ah, I did love this series."

"Me too," I say enthusiastically because I'm suddenly desperate to talk about AZ8. "I love watching AZ8 doing normal non-superstar things like skiing down mountains or eating too much cheese fondue then having a snowball fight."

"Hmm," Dana says.

Hmm? Hmm is not clear at all.

I switch the main light off and my AZ8 Relaxing Stars mood lamp on. But I don't feel relaxed.

Finally, I ask into the dark, "You do still *love* AZ8 deep down, don't you?" I feel so vulnerable, almost like I'm asking Dana if she still loves me!

"Yeah," she answers. "I love AZ8 like I love a smog-free day or those reusable tote bags the Space Agency hands out after the youth conferences."

Hearing this makes my heart feel full, and the icky feeling evaporates. My body relaxes into my comfy bed, and I'm suddenly certain that everything will be OK now that Dana is still a Glow.

In the warm light I can just about make out Dana's face as she rolls to one side and adds, "I love AZ8 like Seri from Lilac Eyes loves a rucksack shaped as a kitten's head." My eyes snap wide. "Goodnight, Skylar."

After a few moments the gentle sound of Dana's snoring confirms she's fallen asleep, but I can't. I lie awake and not even the super squidge of my avocado plushie can lull me to dreamland. And despite the fact I've been awake since 1331BC, I can't stop worrying, not only about my big brother coming home early and discovering Tutankhamun in his bed, but about Dana loving Lilac Eyes and leaving me and AZ8 behind…

5

K-POP MANIA

The next morning, Nana stays at home to prep 70 sweet'n'wild fig and falafel burritos and wait for the Flux-FSCH-88 to arrive, while me, Dana and the formerly dead for 3,000 years Tutankhamun make our way to K-Mania. Oh, and did I mention Kookie my cat is also here? Because for some reason she refuses to leave Tut's arms.

"Let's go up," Dana says, as we board the bus and instantly attract enquiring glances.

Once upstairs, Tut walks to the front, where he stands with his hands on his hips and begins to address all the passengers in his language.

"What's he doing now?" I moan at Dana. "This is not keeping a low profile at all." I make a grab for him, but he shimmies away to carry on his speech. Tut points his cane at a group of intimidating teenagers at the back of the bus and says, "You. You. You. My slave. Slave. Slave. Slave."

"No," I yell. "Stop it."

Dana apologizes to the teens, who huff and puff loudly as I push Tut down in the seat next to her. "Be quiet," I order as I sit behind them.

Tut grins then strokes Kookie's back, seemingly distracted until a few moments later, when he begins to sing. No, not sing, it's more of a high-pitched warble, which seems to get louder and louder with each passing bus stop.

I sink my head into my hands. We're supposed to be incognito!

"There's so much emotion in his voice," Dana says wistfully as she looks back at me with a huge grin on her face. "I wish I knew his language so I could grasp the lyrics."

"I wish I knew his language so I could tell him to shut up," I respond.

"Don't be boring, it's beautiful," Dana chides as she turns to gaze back at Tut. Right then, a light bulb pings in my head. "Translators, that's it." I pull out my phone and open the Chat Around the World language app which I downloaded in case I ever run into a member of AZ8. "Why didn't we think of this sooner?"

I pop my head between them and hold my phone to Tut's mouth. He stops singing immediately.

"It's not going to work, Skylar." Dana shakes her head. "Tut is using a branch of Afro-Asiatic which has long been extinct."

Surely not – languages don't go extinct. "Say something," I instruct Tut.

He swivels around to look me in the eye, then leans into the phone and says, "Slave."

"Not slave," Dana tries again. "*Friend*. We're your friends."

"Come on, Tut," I huff, "say something else?"

Tut pouts at me, then sings the words, "Feta cheeeeese."

I roll my eyes. This is hopeless. The sooner Nana gets the tuk-tuk fixed and we can get rid of Tut, the better.

"I have an idea," Dana says. "How about hieroglyphics?"

"Yes, I remember those. There's like a bird and a lion and a snake and a wibbly-wobbly line and—"

Dana scribbles something in her autograph book and shows it to Tut.

"Hang on," I say, peering at the row of symbols on the page, "you just know hieroglyphics off the top of your head?"

Dana blinks up at me. "'Course. Don't you?"

Tut's eyes scan over the page. He taps his chin thoughtfully, takes the pen and starts drawing.

"Ah. I see," Dana nods. "Interesting. Right. Yes."

"What's he saying?" I stare over his shoulder at the long stream of symbols.

"Hmm. True, true," Dana says to Tut. "I agree. Yes. Right."

"Dana?" I cry, getting annoyed. "Tell me what he's saying."

"Basically, he snuck into the tuk-tuk because he thought it would be, and I quote, *fun time*."

"Fun time?" I snort. "That's ridiculous."

Tut taps on the pad for Dana's attention.

"Also," Dana says, "he's hungry."

"He literally ate half a box of choco hoops and three bagels for breakfast."

Tut rubs his tummy then draws something else.

"Oh." Dana blushes as she reads the next bit. "He needs the toilet and I'm afraid it's a number two situation." She reaches up to press the bell as the K-Mania convention centre shimmers into view. I squeal with delight. Not even an irritating pharaoh can dampen my excitement at making it to this K-pop heaven!

We hop off the bus and make our way over. The

whole place is swarming with K-pop fans, all of us united in our love of great music, snappy dance routines and keyrings which are too large to be sensible. Everyone is dressed in a different kind of uniform depending on which fandom they're part of. As I'm a Glow, which is obviously the best, I'm wearing my AZ8 Wembley T-shirt, dangly earrings and a pair of cute dungarees. Dana's gone for pink jeans and a T-shirt which says *Karbon Neutral K-Pop Fan*.

I must admit, the best dressed fandom is probably the Flossies, who are fans of the very classy girl group, White Teeth. Flossies are always glammed up in high heels, flares and luxurious fabrics.

As we finally get into the convention centre, we spot our German teacher, Herr Schneider, who's a massive Flossy. He's wearing a purple jumpsuit and platform boots. We pretend not to see him, because seeing teachers outside of school is like seeing your parents kiss. Super awkward!

While there's some gentle rivalry between fandoms, sometimes called Fan Wars, we're mostly civil to each other. Except for the fans of Oat Flamingo, an alternative electro-funk-hip-hop-jazz-modern-operatic-R'n'B collective who only the coolest of the cool like. Their fans are called Bad Cakes and are easy to spot because they wear all black, have piercings in strange places and no manners.

"Move it, Glow," a tall girl with a septum piercing shouts as she pushes past me, knocking my precious photobook to the ground.

"Ouch," I say as I rub my sore arm. "Why are the Bad Cakes always in such a foul mood?" I collect my photobook and dust it off.

Tut shakes his fist at the Bad Cakes and Dana giggles at him. "You're so cute," she says.

Tut grins and repeats back – "You're so cute" making Dana's face go bright red.

I take Kookie from Tut's arms and point towards the boys' toilet. Tut stares in the direction of my finger, his face blank. "The toilet is right there," I explain.

"Toilet?" he questions.

"Yes, toilet. You know, for your … hmm." I mime squatting and Tut copies, bending his knees and staring at me with a smile.

"You're so cute," he says again.

"No." I straighten up and look at Dana for help. This time when I squat, I peg my fingers over my nose.

"Ah," Tut cries. "Toilet. Number two situation." He gives me a thumbs up then moonwalks towards the toilets.

I lean my back against the wall and heave a sigh. Finally, one to five minutes of peace and quiet. I take in the beautiful scene around us, the delightful smell of Korean hot dogs and strawberry lip balm, the smiles of a thousand K-pop fans, and the music, just gearing up on the live stage.

Then I notice something that makes me feel anxious all over again.

Lilac Teers.

Their uniform is baggy jeans, belly tops and rucksacks shaped as cat heads. Not that I care, but I've heard cats are *their thing*, with each member being associated with a tiger, leopard, jaguar and domestic tabby.

"Awesome bag," Dana says to one Lilac Teer passing by.

"Ha," I spit. Because yeah sure, the neon pink leopard bag *is* wonderfully cute, but it's nothing compared to the charm of the limited run AZ8 faux fur bag brought out to celebrate the re-re-release of their hit single 'Animal Spots and Human Stripes'.

"Meowww!" someone, definitely not a cat, says and we both turn to see Tut standing beside us, reaching out to touch the cat bag. "Meowww," he repeats.

"Stop," I say, giving him Kookie instead. "Gosh, this is like babysitting."

"Yeah, if your baby was an iconic historical figure," Dana chuckles. "And stop moaning, you love babies."

"It's true," I laugh. "I do love babies."

"You're so cute," Tut says as another Lilac Teer walks past with a leopard bag.

I narrow my eyes at this frankly fabulous piece of fashion. "How do Lilac Eyes have so much merch anyway?" I complain. "They've been around two minutes."

"Because they're amazing," Dana says, scanning the crowd. "Is it just me, or do you feel like you're being watched?"

Funny, because I was thinking the same thing but had put it down to people admiring my artfully applied hair glitter.

A group of Bad Cakes slow in front of us and covertly snap photos. Not of us, but of Tut. Hmm. Interesting.

"Do you think people know?" Dana whispers.

"That's impossible," I say. Because before we left the house, we made Tut look a whole lot less "ancient". While he refused to part with his gold robe, he did accept our suggestion of wearing a pair of shorts under it. We also got him to embrace city-appropriate footwear so he's wearing a pair of my brother's high-top trainers. He looks cool and, with his heavy black eyeliner, he looks almost like a very highly styled K-pop idol.

We walk towards the K-Mania Food Village, and as I'm wondering if it's too early for a triple cheeseburger, my thoughts are shattered by someone squealing, "Ohmygoodness! Everyone, look!" The source of the commotion is a green-haired girl with a Lilac Eyes T-shirt and a very squeaky voice. "Look, look, look!"

I turn to see what everyone has been instructed to look at, but all I see is … Tut?

A group of teenagers from a mix of fandoms approach, all holding out their phones, cameras at the ready.

"Are you in a band?" they ask as they gather around Tut. "Can I find you online?"

"What's your name?"

"I love your gold robe, is it designer?"

"When's your album out?"

Tut grins and then repeats, "Album out." to which everyone coos, causing him to grin even wider.

This is weird – he's literally not doing anything, yet is gathering all this attention. Dana shrugs her shoulders in as much confusion as me.

"You're so cool," the original squeaky voice says, before shoving her phone into Dana's hands. "Here.

Take a photo of me and my friends with him. Everyone say kimchi!"

Dana does as she's told, snapping multiple photos of Tut and his seemingly adoring fans.

"Are you performing here this weekend?" squeaky girl asks Tut.

What a ridiculous question because he's clearly not Korean and therefore not likely to be performing at a Korean pop music convention.

"*Heeeee,*" Tut suddenly sings.

"Oh," Dana says, "he's going to sing again – what a treat!"

"*Leeeee, laaaaa,*" Tut continues, this time wriggling his hips for good measure. "*Wooooo,*" and with this one silky smooth note Tut masters the ultimate boy band move as he clenches his hand and fist pumps the air.

"Not the fist pump," Dana giggles as she blushes along with the growing number of fans surrounding him.

"*Heeeee!*" Tut sings again.

Whoa, he really likes that line.

"*Feta cheeeeese!*"

At this the gathering crowd, who obviously have no taste in music, whoop and cheer.

Tut lifts his lizard-headed cane in the air and shouts, "Good boy! Album out!"

I fold my arms crossly as I watch. "Well, *someone* really does like being the centre of attention."

Dana chuckles. "What do you expect? He's a king back home. Of course he's used to being in the limelight."

Tut moonwalks back and forth and everyone claps for him. Then he stops, spins and cranks his hips. He lifts his index finger and points at me as if beckoning me to dance with him.

I want to, I really do, but after the last time I'm not sure I trust him. I mean, I know I have great moves, but I don't want Tut to shove me again when I inevitably outshine him.

"I think he wants you to join him," Dana says in my ear.

"I know." I sway side to side in time with Tut's funky melody.

"So, go dance." Dana's clicking her fingers and stamping her feet. "Go," she says again. "Stop being so boring."

Boring? How rude. I'm not boring. I could dance this little boy king into the next century if I wanted.

"*Leeeee, laaaaa*," Tut croons as he makes a triple spin.

I waltz towards him and break out my slickest body rolls. I pirouette, cha-cha-cha and do a few robot arms.

"You call this boring?" I shout at Dana.

I close my eyes and get lost in what is sure to be the speediest flossing anyone has ever seen. "You like this?" I yell. "You want more? You want—" Hang on. Why has the singing and stomping stopped? I open my eyes to see Tut now standing still in front of me. He lifts a hand and shoves his palm in my face. I stop moving. "What's wrong?" I ask.

His little face creases in concern and then, in his loudest voice, he announces, "Number two situation."

Everyone bursts into laughter.

"What?" I gasp. "No, it's not. I don't. I mean—" Though everyone is too busy cackling to hear me out. I lower my reddening face. This is so embarrassing.

"He didn't mean it," Dana says as I hide behind her back.

Suddenly, an explosion of green light causes everyone to back up as the tuk-tuk appears right in the middle of our dance circle. For a few weird seconds there's a shocked silence, then Nana sticks her head out and shouts, "The Flux-FSCH-88 was sold out, so I got the Flux-FSCH-55 instead. It's stopped the smoke though the radio is now only playing Portuguese music. Jump in!"

A boy with a long blond ponytail walks up to Nana and says, "Can I have three of your finest chicken kyiv burritos please?"

"No, you cannot," Dana says as she nudges him out of the way to get in the back of the tuk-tuk. "Skylar, Tut, Kookie, let's go."

I dive in the back seat, photobook clasped tight, and squidge over to make space for Tut. But instead of getting in, Tut climbs – yes, climbs – up onto the counter of a bubble tea stall and resumes singing. Kookie pounces right up behind him.

The tuk-tuk's engine roars and Nana, oblivious, shouts, "Belt up: we're going to need optimum speed for this."

"Wait," I say, but my voice is lost to the sound of the revving engine, the clapping crowds and Tut, who is crooning, "*Good boy feta cheeeeese!*" And now Kookie is joining in too. "*Neowww!*"

The tuk-tuk jerks forwards. "Nana, no, wait. Tut," I cry. "Get down!"

"*Feta cheeeeese! Number two situation! Heeeee heeeee!*"

We jerk forward and I reach out to grab for Tut, but I'm still holding my AZ8 photobook and only have one hand to spare. "Dana, help!"

She grabs onto my dungarees, making sure I don't fall out as I reach up as far as I can, my fingers grasping, just about managing to grab the shiny gold material of

Tut's robe as Nana yells over the chaos, "Tuk-tuk take me to the place in my mind's eye."

"Come on, you annoying little show-off!" I shout as the gold fabric rips away.

Tut looks down at the torn cloth in my hand and mouths *"Fun time"* as the portal opens and we dive straight in, leaving the singing ancient pharaoh behind.

6

(NOT SO) ANCIENT EGYPT

This time, I keep my eyes open to take in the bright light, bursting stars and dancing colours of the portal. It's mesmerizing, but after a few seconds – *pop!* – the radiant light is replaced by the overwhelming stench of exhaust fumes. We seem to have landed in the middle of a giant spaghetti junction of roads. Cars, buses and motorbikes whizz by on all sides of the little patch of sun-scorched grass the three of us, plus the tuk-tuk, are perched on.

"This is not it!" Nana yells. She turns her attention to the dashboard and shouts, "Gah! Call yourself a smart speaker! I have cloves of garlic smarter than you."

"Nana, calm down," I try.

"I wanted to go to Egypt," Nana snaps. "I closed my

eyes and pictured it in my mind's eye. Egypt. Egypt. Egypt," she demonstrates, with her eyes squeezed shut.

"And you got Egypt." Dana points to a large blue road sign. On it, in big white lettering, is a swirly bunch of characters I can't read, and under that, in English, the words *Cairo* and *Alexandria*. "It's more that you forgot the ancient part," Dana explains. "This is *present-day* Egypt. Right place, wrong time."

"Ridiculous!" Nana yells so loudly a passing driver thinks she's talking to them and honks their horn.

"What does it matter?" I say, as I grip the torn piece of gold material in my hand. "We don't have Tut with us, anyway. We need to go back to K-Mania and possibly handcuff him. That slippery little monarch."

The tuk-tuk makes a strange wheezing noise and when Nana presses the buttons, nothing happens.

"Everything OK?" I ask, knowing that everything certainly is *not* OK.

Nana grumbles. "I don't know why it's not working. It's hardly been anywhere today. Usually, I can get a good five or six trips out of one batch of fuel."

Dana and I share a knowing look. So, she *has* time travelled before?

Nana gets out and pops open the back of the tuk-tuk. "Ah, silly me," she coos, her rage from seconds ago evaporating. "I put the whatsit in the thingy instead of putting the dingdong in the doodah." I hop out of the tuk-tuk and stand beside her as she slams the boot shut. "It needs twenty minutes to reset itself."

"Nana, tell the truth. Had you ever time travelled before yesterday?"

"No, of course not," she answers, looking at the sky. "It was a fluke. A shock. A complete surprise."

I can't believe she's outright lying to me. My own nana.

She turns away and begins to hum a horrible out-of-tune version of what I would guess is either the national anthem or the jingle from that advert for water filters.

I shove the gold material in my pocket and turn to Dana, who has got down from the tuk-tuk and is fanning herself in the sun.

"Why is this happening?" I ask, in the hope she'll have some answers or at least some Factor 50 sunblock because it's hot out here.

"My personal theory is that there's a tear in the lines of space-time and dark matter. There's also a possibility that the tuk-tuk has warped the—"

"Dana," I groan. "Now is not the time for science."

"Skylar," she says quite seriously, "it is always the time for science. Also, your nana is a hundred per cent lying."

We both turn back to Nana, who I realize is actually humming the Christmas classic "Little Donkey". She stops to say, "I was a donkey in a play once. I can't remember what the play was about. Something about a star or shepherd or—"

"Nana, we deserve to know the truth," I say in my most authoritative voice. "What's going on?"

She doesn't answer, only shrugs, and not in a way that suggests she doesn't know what's happening. "I am just as confused as you are," Nana says in the sweet old lady voice I've heard her use when she wants someone to carry her shopping home.

"We don't believe you. And we won't stop interrogating you until you tell us the truth, the whole truth and nothing but the truth."

Nana waves a ziplock bag full of dark golden slivers in front of our faces. "Dried mango?"

"Ooh, yes please," Dana says as she takes the bag and digs in. Nana dries her own mango above the washing machine in our kitchen and there's something about the essence of fabric conditioner that makes it truly tasty.

"I can't get enough of this sweet, leathery goodness," Dana says.

"Hard agree," I mumble, while grappling with a particularly sticky piece wedged between my front teeth. "Hang on. No, no, no! Nana's buying us off again. First cash, now dried fruit. What next, screen time?"

Now, Nana looks super guilty. "I don't know what you're talking about, Skylar. I'm just a simple old woman with a food truck, trying to make my way in the world."

"Ooh, ooh, ooh." Dana jumps as her phone pings in her pocket. "It's an alert from K-Mania. Darcy Delaney is doing a livestream. At least we can keep up with what's going on, even if we are over 3,500 miles away."

She clicks on the link and Darcy appears with her pink candyfloss hair spread out like a halo, a rainbow of eyeshadow and earrings shaped as tiny calculators.

"Her style is just chef's kiss," Dana says.

"I know. She's so cool."

"Hey peeps, it's your girl, Darcy Delaney from K-popdontstop.com, your one-stop shop for all K-pop news, reviews and possible untruths. I'm here at K-Mania because, unlike most of you, I got a VIP ticket with full backstage access. Now of course K-Mania is not the same this year without AZ8 and their crazy fans."

Crazy?

"Yes, that's right, the Glows are crying sparkly little tears since the boy band announced they were breaking up."

I growl because, while Darcy may look cool, she's

not acting very cool right now. Also, AZ8 never said they were breaking up. They said they were taking a break.

"I get it, guys," Darcy says to the camera. "I too dedicated my life to AZ8 but let's step back and ask ourselves, were they really *that* great?"

This truly offensive suggestion causes me to launch at the phone. "Why, you snooty, flamingo-haired, well-dressed—"

"Stop" Dana moves her phone away from me. "I'm trying to listen."

"It's time to move on, you bores," Darcy barks.

Bores?

"Why does anything good ever need to move on?" I mumble. Moving on is sad and unnecessary. If it were up to me things would stay the same always, with everyone doing what they've always done.

Dana is still superglued to Darcy's livestream of meanness.

"Of course, this year the K-Mania crowd is only here for one thing and that's—"

The limited-edition AZ8 wooden chopping board, I think. Surely that was everyone's sole purpose for getting a ticket. But no, Darcy takes a breath and shouts, "Lilac Eyes!"

Dana lets out a whoop and does a little happy dance with her arms.

"Yes, that's right. The new girl group sensation is set to perform live at K-Mania tomorrow afternoon, so if you're interested in seeing K-pop history, or even better, meeting your girl Darcy – that's me! – then get yourselves down here to beg for a ticket."

"Enough," I say, as I stomp to the edge of the grassy verge, sit down and sulk. Luckily, I have my AZ8 photobook tucked down the front of my dungarees, which gives me some much-needed comfort. I can't believe Dana hasn't asked to see it yet. Especially when she knows I spent three whole weekends putting all 1,276 photocards in alphabetical order. *A* for astronaut-related photoshoots, *B* for beach-related photoshoots, *C* for circus-related photoshoots – I especially love the ones of Haru juggling. I caress the pages then flick to my most favourite section: *I* for infants, with the special-edition photocards of each member as a baby.

Eventually Darcy must end her livestream as Dana comes over and sits next to me. "Here," she says, offering the last piece of fruit leather.

I decline, because I don't want to get my photobook sticky.

Dana leans over my shoulder, where I'm now on *M*

for medical-related photoshoots. I point to a particularly special photocard. "Remember when Jungwon cracked a tooth while doing a double somersault on the European leg of the Grow in the Arms of Love tour?"

"Not really," Dana says slowly.

So now she doesn't even remember monumental moments in pop history? This has gone too far.

"Why do things always have to change, Dana? First my mum is away at all these conferences, and then my dad is training all the time and can't watch Gardeners' World, then Nana is super busy with her food deliveries, and then AZ8 want a break and now you…"

"Now me what?" she says as she pushes her hair off her warm face. "I haven't changed. I'm not going anywhere."

"You have. You will."

"This is life, Skylar. Things happen. We move on."

Nana comes over and with great effort and many creaks and cricks lowers herself to the grass to sit on the other side of me. She taps a photo of Dig-D eating a bowl of spicy squid soup. "Ah, I like this one. Good to see young people eating squid."

"Yes, this is the S section," I say. "S for snacks, soups and seafood-related photoshoots. It's one of the biggest sections in the book."

Nana strokes my hair, then stops when she notices how much glitter is in it. "I'm sorry your boy band broke up, Skylar."

"They're not broken up," I say through gritted teeth. "They're having a break."

"Of course they are." She pats my leg. "The tuk-tuk's ready to go now."

"Hang on," I say. "You still haven't told us the truth."

"Yeah, Nana," Dana says with a sassy snap of her head.

"The truth?" Nana says, while dodging eye contact. "The truth is, I love you very much."

"The truth about the tuk-tuk," Dana says in her Dana-means-business voice.

Nana looks up at the sky. "Ooh, look. A big aeroplane."

"Stop it," I snap.

Nana puts a hand to her forehead and says, "I'm just a simple old woman full of innocence—"

"Enough!" I cry. "Tell us the truth."

Nana sits up straight, crosses and then uncrosses her legs. She checks her nails, then picks at a loose rhinestone on her jeans. She struggles to stand up and then walks away from us. We follow. Then, finally, she gives in.

"Oh, all right. I'm doing what all foodies do. Travelling and collecting recipes. Sampling different cuisines. Finding the best ingredients. Every foodie travels the world for inspiration," she shrugs. "I travel time instead."

Dana scoffs. "This is wild. Did you invent it yourself?"

Nana lets out an almost crazed-sounding laugh. "Don't be ridiculous. I bought it from Akua."

"Your pet rabbit from childhood?" I ask, completely confused.

"No, silly. Akua from the dental surgery. Did you know she's allergic to eggs? And parrots? How strange. Still, she's a great saleswoman. I also bought a chiffon dress from her—"

"Moving on," Dana says impatiently.

"At first, I thought the tuk-tuk was fabulous." Nana smiles. "But the problem is, it has limits."

"I thought so." Dana takes out her phone, ready to type notes. "And these limits are?"

Nana taps her chin and answers, "It gets confused easily, like Skylar when she's hungry."

I can't deny it, I am a person who gets mighty confused when snacks are in short supply.

"And as you saw yesterday," Nana continues, "it

sleeps overnight. However, the main issue is, when you're directing it, you need to have a crystal-clear picture in your mind's eye of where you want it to go, or stuff like this happens..." She gestures to our modern-day Egypt surroundings.

"That's it?" Dana asks.

"That's it," Nana says, "Now, let's go back to KidZania."

"K-Mania," I correct as I jump in the back seat.

Dana slides in beside me then gasps at something on her phone. "Erm, Skylar, you might want to look at this." She shows me the search results for the hashtag K-Mania and the top trending topics are #DebutIdol #VoiceOfAGeneration and #IdolCat. There's also a photo of Tut, grinning ear to ear and holding up Kookie, surrounded by a huge crowd of people.

"He's having fun?" I ask, shocked.

"That's great to hear," Nana says. "He's a good boy."

Dana hits like on the photo. "It warms my heart to think of Tut being happy for once in his short existence. It's what he wanted after all: *fun time*."

"He deserves it," Nana says as the tuk-tuk revs.

What are they both on about?

I click my seat belt and tug my photobook under it. "He's a literal king back home. Crowns and thrones and gold and adoring subjects – his whole existence is *fun time*."

"Except," Dana wobbles her head, "it wasn't, was it? Don't you remember anything you learned about ancient Egyptian history?"

"Of course I do – I remember making a canopic jar out of paper cups and gold paint."

Dana rolls her eyes at me. "Skylar, he's younger than us and is already responsible for reversing the religiopolitical rules put in place by his predecessor."

"Is that bad?" I'm not sure if religiopolitical is something fun or not.

"It's a lot of pressure. Plus, he was put on the throne at nine years old. What were you doing at nine years old?"

"She was making a whole lot of mess and noise," Nana laughs from the front seat. "Like any other kid."

"Exactly!" Dana chuckles. "I was crazy at nine too, solving complex equations and reading Tolstoy."

We look again at the photo on Dana's phone on which someone has commented:

Living our best life #bff #bestdayever #funtime #fetacheese

"Such a shame we have to end this," Dana says.

"Unless…" Nana swings around to look at us, a single eyebrow raised.

"Unless what?" I ask, trying and failing to lift a single eyebrow too.

"Unless we leave him there for a little while longer? You see, there's a short stop-off I've been wanting to make ever since I started travelling this way. But I keep getting nervous and turkeying out. Maybe with you two guarding the tuk-tuk I could finally feel brave enough to do it."

"Do what?" I ask.

"There's a particular dish I can't stop thinking about. I've tried to recreate it many times, but it's never worked. I think if I can taste it one more time, I'll be able to replicate it. It will only take a minute. I'm sure,"

Nana makes a compelling case. "What do you think, Dana? What is your genius brain telling you?"

Dana ponders this and then says, "I think leaving King Tutankhamun in the present day, for a short period of time, at a K-pop convention where he's gathering attention and online traction, seems like a perfectly fine idea."

I nod in agreement, then lean forward and tap Nana on the shoulder. "It's cool, Nana. We can look after the tuk-tuk while you— Waaaa!" I yell as Nana slams the big red button.

7

THE BUTTERFLY
EFFECT

We land in a wide-open green space with scrubby grass.
There are a couple of trees, a cluster of bushes and in the
distance a pale pink house. There's something familiar
about this place, but I can't put my finger on it.

Nana's rhinestone jeans glitter in the sun as she
hops out of the tuk-tuk. "Now, you girls sit tight while
I pop in that house over there and get something."
She checks her reflection in the wing mirror. "How
do I look?"

"Depends," Dana says. "What look are you going for?"

Nana straightens her headwrap. "I want to look like
a mysterious stranger."

Dana nods. "Then you nailed it."

Nana's hands shake as she leans in to grab her recipe

notepad from the glove box. She stares down at it and smiles widely. "This is it," she says.

"This is what?" I ask, but it's too late, Nana's already skipping off towards the house. I've never seen her move so fast before. How weird. Though I guess *weird* is the theme of this weekend.

We sit and wait for her to come back.

We wait and wait, and then we wait some more.

Dana sighs. I sigh. She sighs again, I sigh again, and then we both sigh in unison.

I stare at my phone and the dreaded words of No Internet Connection. "How *did* people pass the time before having a constant video stream of animals being hilarious?"

"It's a mystery," Dana says as she too gazes sadly at her own pointlessly unconnected device.

We talk dreamily of our favourite online content – AZ8 for me and podcasts on climate change for her – until we run out of things to say.

"This is boring," I say.

"So boring," Dana agrees.

A big orange butterfly nears the tuk-tuk and, because there's absolutely nothing else to do, we watch it make loops. Its natural beauty prompts me to sing AZ8's underrated classic, "My Heart Flutters When You Say Hi".

Dana groans. "That's AZ8's worst song."

"AZ8 don't have bad songs," I say, completely outraged.

"Yes, they do. And it's that one. I don't know why anyone would write a whole song about such a sinister little insect. Urgh." She shivers into my side as the butterfly drifts towards us. "Don't let it land on me!"

I can't help but giggle.

"Don't laugh at my phobia, Skylar."

"I'm not," I say, definitely laughing. "Look, it's going now."

I feel Dana relax as the pretty butterfly flutters towards a bush a few metres away from us.

"Dana, if you could time travel anywhere, where would you go?"

"I wouldn't," she answers, her eyes tracking the butterfly.

"I bet you'd want to go back and stop whoever invented cars or nuclear energy."

A small smile quirks on one side of her mouth. "Tempting, but no."

"Or you'd want to find tyrants and dictators from history and lock them up in a cupboard."

"No," Dana says, tensing as the butterfly returns and lands on the dashboard. "Why is it staring at me?" she whines.

"It's not staring at you," I laugh. "Come on, Dana, think of how much better the world would be if we could positively educate all the bad people of the past. We could, like, hmm…" I carefully consider options more mature than locking tyrants in cupboards. "I know, we could make them listen to AZ8's *How to Show the World You Love It* album and then read them English translations of the lyrics."

Dana smiles for a second, then her face becomes serious. "Don't you know anything about how to time travel safely?"

I think this over. "Wear a seat belt?" I try.

Dana rolls her eyes at me and laughs. "The number one rule about going back in time is that you don't change anything. You don't touch anything. You don't talk to anyone, and you certainly don't play music from the future."

"Even when the lyrics are super profound statements on the way we live in the world today?" I say while making a heart with my fingers.

"*Especially* when the lyrics are super profound statements on the way we live in the world today."

"What's the point of going back in time if you're not going to interact with cool people, invest in cryptocurrency or warn the residents of Pompeii about the whole volcanic eruption thing?" I shake my head, confused.

"Funnily enough," Dana says as she points at the butterfly on the dashboard, "it's known as the butterfly effect. Obviously, it's a terrible name, but it's based on the theory that if you went back in time and changed one tiny thing it could alter the entire course of history." Dana continues, "Imagine if a butterfly flaps its wings in Brazil, it could cause a ripple in the air that days or even weeks later becomes a tornado in Texas."

As though the butterfly knows it's being talked about, it lifts off the dashboard and heads towards us. I could watch butterflies in flight all day: the way they move is so relaxing. But as it hovers between us, Dana shatters the peace, yelling, "Go away, you four-winged weirdo!" She flips her red hair back and forth until the poor little creature takes refuge on my side of the back seat.

Flustered, but content that the butterfly isn't coming near her, Dana continues her explanation. "Imagine your time machine crash-lands in the middle of a road and blocks traffic, which then makes the buses run late, which then means Haru never makes it to that first ever AZ8 audition?"

At this, I gasp. The story of Haru almost missing

the audition for AZ8 is legendary. His parents' car had broken down so he had to get a bus, which only got him there at the very last minute!

"So…" I ponder, carefully processing this awful scenario. "What you're saying is, we *can* time travel as long as we don't play any AZ8 music to dictators, look at any butterflies, or stop Haru from getting on a bus?"

The butterfly begins to circle us and Dana tries to duck out of the way.

"It's a little more complicated than that," she says. "But yes— Argh! Will this creature please get out of my face while I'm trying to explain science?" Dana grabs my photobook and whacks at the air, violently smashing the butterfly against the roof.

We lock eyes. What did she just do? Slowly, Dana lowers the photobook and we both peer up at the orange splat.

Dana pants. "Oh my Malala Yousafzai!" She puts her hand over her mouth, goes completely pale and declares, "I've destroyed history."

I look at the squished butterfly and picture an army of tornadoes looping across the world. This is bad. This is very bad.

"I'm an awful person!" Dana wails. "I'm a super villain."

"Calm down," I try. "Breathe." But it doesn't work.

Dana is now crying, and not just any crying, she's snot bubble crying.

"I'm evil. I'm worse than those people who take private jets and leave their litter on beaches."

Tears are flooding down her face and I feel awful. Not just for my best friend, who is in a horrible state, but for the butterfly. I need to do something. I need to...

"I have an idea!" I climb in the front seat. "I can fix this."

"Skylar," Dana whimpers from the back. "Are you going to do something impulsive?"

I'm not impulsive, I think, as I hit the big red button, which I'm 50 per cent sure is the start button.

The tuk-tuk whirs to life. Honestly, I'm a little scared, but I know Dana: she won't be able to live with herself if a bunch of cows get swept up in tornadoes because of her butterfly killing actions.

The tuk-tuk lurches forward, then just as Nana did, I say, "Tuk-tuk, please take me to the place in my mind's eye." I close my eyes and picture our current location, but it's no good. We're still here.

Ah, I know. "Tuk-tuk, please rewind ten minutes to the place in my mind's eye."

It lurches again, then it gets going, trundling along until it hits a rock and bounces, like a rickety old ghost train. The tuk-tuk speeds up as the portal appears in front of us. I squeal with delight: it's working! Suddenly the whole thing launches into the air as it hits yet another bump, and my photobook, which was lying unsecured on the back seat, flies up and out.

"Grab it!" I shout as we smash back down and race towards the light. Dana reaches up to catch the photobook, but suddenly we're enveloped in the warm shining glow of the portal…

Arggghhh! "There's no going back now!" I shout, except going back is exactly the point of what I'm trying to do. I'm terrified by the millions of possibilities, not to mention the one very real possibility that I've lost my photobook!

I lift my hands off the wheel and squeeze my eyes shut. The light is way more intense when I'm driving than when I was the passenger: it sparkles like when you drink a fizzy drink too fast and it goes up your nose.

Pop!

We land with a bump, and everything goes still.

Nervously, I blink open my eyes.

We're not, as I feared, in the middle of a face-off between two T-rexes or the battle of Troy; we're back exactly where we were. In the tuk-tuk. And I'm *back in the back seat* next to Dana.

I look at her, she looks at me and our mouths fall open.

"Now, you girls sit tight while I pop in that house over there and get something." Nana's voice causes us both to jump. Where did she come from? She was all the way in that pastel-coloured house, yet now she's here, standing outside the tuk-tuk and checking her reflection in the wing mirror. "How do I look?" she asks.

At our stunned silence, Nana's eyes flick up to us. I poke Dana into action.

"Depends," Dana says, her voice doing that strange thing it does when we're in Drama class, which is the only subject she is consistently bad at. "What look are you going for?" She turns to me and squeezes one eye shut.

"What's wrong with your eye?" I whisper.

"I'm winking at you," Dana says. "Letting you know I'm in on what's happening here."

"You mean about us reliving our lives?" I whisper back.

"Huh?" Nana asks, confused at all the hushed communication taking place.

"Nothing, Nana."

Nana straightens her headwrap and says, "I want to look like a mysterious stranger."

"Then you nailed it," Dana replies while nudging me and repeating her weird scary wink.

Nana's hands shake as she leans in to grab her recipe notepad from the glove box. She stares down at it and smiles widely. "This is it," she says. Then she skips off … again!

"I can't believe this is happening," I say.

"Me neither. We actually went back in time! You righted my wrongs." Dana throws her arms around me. "I will never smoosh a butterfly again. And look—" She gestures to my lap where my precious photobook has returned. I hug it to my chest. "Oh, I'm so happy. I thought I'd lost you."

Dana blows out a breath. "Whoa! I really thought only your nana could time travel. It's crazy dangerous that this mighty power is so easily transferable. Imagine what would happen if it got into the wrong hands and— Urgh, it's back!" Dana ducks as the butterfly, which is essentially back from the dead, flies straight at her.

"Don't squish it," I warn her.

Dana's eyes follow the butterfly around the tuk-tuk. "How can your tiny body support such big wings?" she howls at the creature. "Oh, Skylar, I really want to squish it."

I take her hand and squeeze it as the butterfly gets up close and personal. "You're doing really well, Dana. I believe in you."

"Yuck, yuck, yuck," Dana gags. "I bet you were cuter as a caterpillar."

A few minutes later, the butterfly flies out into the world, off to enjoy it's life, unsquished. I give Dana a high five, then sit back in my seat and sigh. That was intense. "I can't believe the time travel element of the tuk-tuk is so easy to operate."

"Yeah," Dana agrees. "Looked easy."

"Easy peasy, lemon squeezy, knock your kneeses."

"Not that we'd ever do that again," Dana says, as she puts a hand on my shoulder and laughs.

"No, of course not. We only time travelled just now as a matter of emergency."

"I know. It's not like we'd ever do it for … personal gain."

"Or fun," I add.

"Or to broaden our horizons."

"Or to eat a whole roast chicken with our bare hands like a true ye olden days peasant," I say as I mimic tearing meat with my teeth.

Dana laughs. "Is that really what you'd choose to do?"

I shrug because I haven't thought about it properly. "I don't know. But maybe we *should* do something."

Dana narrows her eyes at me. "Even though time travelling could be dangerous for humanity?"

"We're not dangerous." I climb into the front seat, then say, "Why don't *you* choose a time period to visit?" I turn to see her reaction. Her bottom lip wobbles and her eyes pass over the dashboard. "We can't," she says, her nose scrunching. "We can't, we can't, we ... hmm." Then, she clambers up front to sit next to me.

"Yes!" I shout.

"One quick trip," she says, very seriously, with a finger in the air.

"Woo-hoo!"

"Though eating ye olden days chicken isn't the most exciting. Not when you consider there's over 5,000 years of recorded human history to explore."

She's right. I could eat a whole roast chicken at home, I don't need to time travel for it. "So, where to?" I ask.

"Preferably somewhere without butterflies. You choose. I know you'll choose something we'll both like."

Something we'll both like? Whoa, the pressure is on. Before yesterday it would have been simple.

But ever since Dana came out as a Lilac Teer everything is different. Though, if she's trusting me now, that must mean deep down she's still my bestie and is happy for me to pick something AZ8 related.

I hit the red button, look at Dana and smile, because despite what's happened over the last 24 hours, or centuries, we're still besties and we still think the same. There's only one place to go. As the tuk-tuk speeds up I close my eyes and take my hands off the wheel.

8

THE BABYSITTERS CLUB

We land in the small courtyard of a cute brown house. There are plant pots everywhere and wind chimes hang from a low roof covered in black tiles, which curl up in each corner. The wind chimes tinkle in a gentle breeze and little birds sing as they hop from one plant to another.

This is it. It's exactly how it was in the 21-part documentary *The Origins of AZ8*.

I jump down from the tuk-tuk, head towards the front door and kick off my shoes, adding them to a pile of plastic sandals and trainers beside the door. Dana copies.

"Where are we?" she asks.

"I think you know," I tease.

She grins. "I think I know too, but I don't want to get excited in case what I know isn't actually what you think I know."

I take her by the shoulders and shake her. "We're in Korea!"

Dana does her happy dance. "Yes! This is cooler than the time I went to the recycling plant and got to see how they separate the glass from the paper."

I've heard Dana gush about her trip to the recycling plant more than her family holiday to Disney World, so I know I've chosen correctly. "I've brought us here," I say proudly, "to the birthplace of our leaders, AZ8."

Suddenly the front door slides open and a stressed looking woman, wearing a lot of blue denim, steps out. "*Annyeonghaseyo!*" she says as she beckons us in.

Inside the house looks, disappointingly, kind of like my own. There's washing drying on a clothes rack, a messy dining table covered in papers and books, empty teacups and more plant pots.

The woman bustles about as she talks to us in fast Korean. She gestures to me, then Dana, the whole time talking, talking, talking. She picks up a notepad and hands it to us, but of course neither of us can read the language. She then walks off into another part of the house, chattering away to herself.

"Why are there no subtitles?" I say under my breath. Despite the colossal amount of Korean content I consume, I only know a handful of Korean words.

The woman returns, this time with a baby's bottle in one hand and a large pack of nappies in the other. She hands Dana the bottle and me the nappies. There's more talk, more pointing at various things and finally she says, "*annyeonghi gyeseyo.*"

"Ooh," I say excitedly. "That means goodbye. She's saying goodbye to us."

The woman puts on her jacket, which is also blue denim, gives us a little bow and walks out.

"Did you see?" I ask Dana. "She left, so I was right. *annyeonghi gyeseyo* does mean goodbye. Because she just left." I chortle, thoroughly impressed with my own foreign language skills.

"It's like she thought we were babysitters or something." Dana stares at the baby's bottle in her hand, then turns to me and cautiously asks, "Why are we here?"

I'm so glad she asked. "I wanted to pick a perfect moment in history. So, I thought of the two things I love most."

It's obvious, so why does Dana, who is my bestie and the person who knows me better than anyone in the world, still look so puzzled?

She clears her throat. "OK, continue…"

I bounce excitedly. "I thought of my ultimate AZ8 bias: Tae." I put the nappies down and point at Tae's perfectly smouldering face on my T-shirt.

"Yes…" Dana nods slowly.

"And…" I do an imaginary drumroll. "Babies!"

"Babies?" Dana's expression is weird. Like a strange combination of angry eyebrows, shocked eyes and baffled mouth. But I don't have time to dissect her feelings right now because there's a murmuring sound coming from the other room. That must be him! I'm so excited I break into a shoulder bounce and double spin.

"Let's go!" I say as I grab Dana by the arm and pull her through to the other room. And there, lying in a frilly white crib is the sweetest little baby I've ever seen in my life. "Baby Tae," I coo.

"You didn't!" Dana says, completely incredulous.

"Baby Tae," I repeat, this time on the verge of tears because of the cuteness overload. "Boojoo boojoo!"

Tae's chubby little feet stick out of his tartan baby grow. "Look at his fat little toes!" I giggle. "It's crazy to think as a grown-up he's a Taekwondo Grand Master."

Dana throws her hands up and groans. "Skylar, why on earth would you time travel to see your AZ8 bias as a baby?"

"Because I love babies. And I wanted to see if Tae already had dimples when he was a little sheesh-moo."

"Sheesh-moo?" she repeats, her tone inappropriately sharp. "I very much doubt that's a real word."

"Are you sure? Because I think I've seen it in the dictionary. Right next to a photograph of this little boogie boogie boo."

Dana puts her hands on her head and the anger drips down her whole face.

I turn back to the little sheesh-moo and whoa, I've never seen Tae's hair so healthy. I almost feel bad for the years of blow-drying, backcombing and dyeing it's going to be subjected to in the name of K-pop boy band fashion. I reach down to gently stroke it. "Softer than kitten's fur."

"Stop touching him!" Dana snaps. "We are not to touch anything from the past."

I pull my hand away guiltily. Baby Tae wriggles and murmurs, then his murmurs turn into a cry. I look at Dana's furious face, then I look back at the crying baby Tae. There's only one thing for it. I lift him out of the crib. "Come here, you little cutie patootie."

"What are you doing?" Dana squeals.

"He needs a cuddle," I say, holding him to me gently.

"No, he doesn't."

I sniff his hair. "Ooh, he smells delightful." I hold him out to Dana. "Smell him."

"No, I will not smell him," Dana says as she ducks away. "Put. Him. Down."

How can she be so cold-hearted? No baby is left crying – not on my watch. I walk around the room and rock baby Tae in my arms. I even hum a little bit of AZ8's smash hit single, "Hot Feet". *"Ooh, your toes are dancing; I love it when they're dancing."*

"Skylar, stop that right now!" Dana's sharp tone is clearly stressing baby Tae as his cries get louder and louder.

"Shush," I tell her.

"This situation is very weird and I'm very uncomfortable."

"Ooh, hot feet, don't stop moving." I carry on, but it's not helping: he starts to fuss and fidget in my arms, squawking more like a bald eagle on a wildlife programme than a future singing sensation.

Maybe he's hangry. I grab the bottle from Dana and try to feed him, but he turns his face away and cries even harder. "Pfft," I sigh, defeated. "What does he want?"

"Maybe he needs his nappy changed," she offers. "Smell his bum."

"What?!" I shriek. "I'm not going to smell baby Tae's bum."

"The lady gave us the nappies for a reason."

"Waaaaaaaa!" Baby Tae is really showing us what his superior vocal cords can do, and it's probably the only sound he'll ever make I don't want to hear.

And again, even louder. "WAAAAAAAA!"

It's brain splitting.

Dana puts her fingers in her ears.

"Shhh, shhh," I try. His face is damp with tears, his chubby little feet kicking and shoving. This is stressful. "Say if there's something really wrong with him?" I panic. "Say if he cries so much, he damages his vocal cords and is unable to sing in later life. Say if I've drawn too much attention to his chubby baby feet which causes him to feel ashamed and never go on to write and perform "Hot Feet", the song that changed my life." I can't even begin to wrap my head around what this all means. It's far too mind-boggling. "Say if—"

"Stop!" Dana shouts over the wailing.

Then, silence.

It's a miracle. Dana's shout has caused baby Tae to stop crying. Even Dana no longer looks quite so furious. Baby Tae looks over at her, his bottom lip turns out ... then, "WAAAAAAAA!"

"Maybe he needs some fresh air?" I say as I carry him back through the living room and out into the courtyard where the tuk-tuk is parked.

Oh, I know. I slide in the front seat and with my free hand grab the photobook and flip it open to V for AZ8 with various stunning hairstyles. "Look, baby Tae, look how much blue hair suits you."

Baby Tae's teary eyes focus on the picture for a few seconds, and he calms down.

"He likes it," I call to Dana as she grabs our shoes and comes over.

I point to a photocard of Tae and Woojin with matching purple mullets and explain, "This hairstyle is to symbolize the two sides of your personality. Business in the front, party in the back." At this, he gurgles. "See," I say to Dana. "Look how much he enjoys seeing photos of himself."

"The baby's a narcissist," Dana mumbles as she sits on a plastic stool.

I continue to flick through the photocards, baby Tae delighted with his own image and me super happy to finally share my photobook with someone who's actually interested.

"I'm really uncomfortable with baby Tae sitting in a literal time machine," Dana says.

"Why? It's not like he's going to drive it anywhere," I laugh. "1, 2, 3, go!" I say as I pretend to drive the tuk-tuk. Tae giggles and claps. I do it again, "1, 2, 3, go!"

More belly laughs.

No wonder Tae's mum assumed I was the babysitter: I'm a natural born entertainer. Kids love me.

"1, 2, 3, go!"

Tae's really giggling and gurgling now.

Dana groans. "This is so boring. I can't believe you made us time travel twenty years into the past and all the way to Korea to entertain a *baby*. Boring!"

Why is Dana being so mean? Dana of a few days ago would've loved this, wouldn't she? Or is she right? *Am I boring?*

No, she's wrong: this moment is perfect – though, I'll be honest, babysitting the future of pop is tiring. I lean back and close my eyes for a few moments while baby Tae sits on my lap and pretends to play with the steering wheel.

The tuk-tuk's engine suddenly revs. My eyes snap open. The dashboard is lit up; Baby Tae must have pressed something. "No, no," I tell him. "No driving time machines." I reach forward to press the lilac button to switch the power off, but instead the lights flash and the horn honks. Baby Tae bubbles with excitement.

I try the green switch, the yellow knob and the white dial, but nothing. "Why won't this thing switch off?" I hit the blue button and a Portuguese pop song plays.

"Let me help," Dana says, as she slides in the front seat next to us. "Tuk-tuk," she says into the speaker, "please stop."

The three dots on the dashboard flash and it replies, "Sorry. I don't recognize your voice."

Dana gasps in offense. "Oh, yes, you do," she shouts back.

"Waaa!" a voice says from the entranceway of the courtyard. We turn to see a teenage girl in a sparkly pink velour tracksuit.

"Yikes!" Dana's eyes go wide. "That must be the *real* babysitter." We both face the girl and say, "Hello," as innocently as possible.

The girl walks towards us and shouts, "*Aniyo!*" Which, with my limited language skills, I can only assume means, "Who are you and why are you stealing my babysitting work?"

"Uh-oh!" Dana panics. "We need to get out of here before we create another squished butterfly situation."

I lean close to the mic and say, "Tuk-tuk," but baby Tae wriggles around in my arms, brings his wet lips to the mic and says, "1, 2, 3, GO!"

The lights flicker off and on and the tuk-tuk lurches forward. I grab the steering wheel but because I'm eleven and completely unskilled in the act of steering – seriously, you should see me on the go-karts – I can only make the tuk-tuk turn right, right and right again, creating a sort of loop.

"Stop this!" Dana squeals as her shoulder bashes into mine.

"I'm trying!" I howl as I attempt to grip the steering wheel, my photobook and baby Tae, who is now chuckling like this is the funniest thing to ever have happened.

Right, right and right again we go while the babysitter stands in the middle, her face etched with confusion. And, to be fair, it is a pretty confusing situation.

"What should I do?" I shout at Dana, though the shouting is unnecessary given that her ear is pressed against my face.

"Motion sickness!" Dana wails, rather unhelpfully, as baby Tae suddenly breaks into an ear-splitting cry. So now, the tuk-tuk is looping, baby Tae is screaming, and Dana's stomach is audibly churning.

The smell of burning rubber hits my nostrils and I am forced to weigh up two very real and very unwanted outcomes. A: the tuk-tuk's wheels wear down, it breaks, and we're trapped not only on the other side of the world, but a decade before we were even meant to be born. Or B: I take a baby back to the future with me, and AZ8 never form.

I need to get rid of this baby! There's only one thing for it. I try to recall everything our PE teacher, Coach Cathy, has ever taught me about overarm throws. I take a breath and whisper into Tae's tiny ear, "Goodbye, sweet singing angel." Then, with all my might and strength, I chuck that little baby right out of the tuk-tuk. He flies through the sky and lands straight into the babysitter's arms.

"Tuk-tuk," I say, desperately picturing my house, "please take me to the place in my mind's eye."

9

TEMPTATION

"That was fun," I hoot, as we land outside of my house. Home again. Everything looks just as we left it, I notice with relief.

"That was horrendous." Dana holds out her hands. "Look, I'm shaking." She hops out of the tuk-tuk and drops into downward dog.

"What are you doing?"

"Yoga," she says, her voice muffled. "My body has never had to deal with this much excess adrenaline."

I check my own hands and yep, they're also a little shaky. I step down from the tuk-tuk and mirror Dana's movements. The blood rushes to my head – what a lovely sensation. Already I'm starting to feel calmer.

I look at Dana, who's all red-faced and puffy, and I burst out laughing.

"What?" she snaps.

"You look so weird upside down."

She tries to frown but it just makes her look even stranger.

"Stop laughing!" she demands, but once she stands upright, she's chuckling too, and now we've both got the giggles.

"I can't believe you chucked Tae from a moving vehicle," she says. "That was such a distressing experience. I think it's given me a grey hair. And red heads aren't genetically conditioned to go grey."

"This adventure is wild," I say quietly, in case any of my nosy neighbours overhear. "Where to next?"

Dana lifts a finger and waggles it. "No way."

No? She can't be serious – this is so much fun. "Come on, Dana." If anything proves I'm not boring, it's this!

She takes a big breath and steadies herself into tree pose.

"You don't want a little peek back in time?" I try. "A passing glance? A fleeting look? A quick peek-a-boo?"

"No," she says sternly. She switches legs and I do too. "Whoa, your balance is A class, Skylar."

"I know." I drop into eagle pose. "But we're not talking about my freakish levels of flexibility and focus right now, we're talking about our next adventure.

Think of how much fun that troublesome little pharaoh is having at K-Mania. We should be allowed to have some fun too. Especially as we're the ones who broke him out of Mummyville in the first place."

"Don't try to tempt me," Dana says as she gently lowers herself down into eagle. "I'm untemptable." She takes a deep breath, though I notice her eyes are continually darting to the tuk-tuk, so much so that she wobbles and falls out of position.

She's fighting it. I can tell.

I sigh longingly. "I wonder what the atmosphere was like in parliament the day the government banned plastic straws…"

Dana makes a slight mewing noise as she turns away from the tuk-tuk.

I keep pushing. "It was probably as electric as it was the same day Greta Thunberg did her first ever school strike. Can you imagine what it would feel like to be there?"

Dana looks like she might explode.

"Or when Galileo perfected the telescope…" I whisper.

"I can't do this!" Dana yells, as she climbs in the front seat. "I was wrong. I'm tempt-able, I'm very much tempt-able."

"Woo-hoo," I applaud. "So where to? Are there any smart people you want to meet in real life?"

"I thought you'd never ask."

"Einstein? Da Vinci? Frida Kahlo? That guy who won the air fryer on the Ten Questions quiz show?"

She laughs. "You know me so well."

Hearing this makes me warm inside, because despite her being a Lilac Teer, she's still my bestie and I *do* know her inside out.

She gets out her phone. "Here's a handy list I call Dana's top idols of science, technology and general brilliance of mind, updated version 2.7. Now let me think this through." She goes quiet as she reads and I hop in the front of the tuk-tuk.

"I'm very tempted by Frida Kahlo," Dana mumbles. "But then, Gertrude Ederle? Vera Atkins?"

"Come on, choose already."

Dana bites her fingernails and mumbles, "Boudicca? Ooh, that could be cool. Hmm, let me look at version 2.3 instead. I'm sure there were—"

I groan. "We don't have time for this. I mean, we do, we have all the time there's ever been in the world. But the quicker you decide, the quicker we go on our adventure and the quicker we can whip back around to K-Mania to scoop up the good merch."

"OK," she says, tucking her phone back in her pocket. "I've decided."

"Awesome. I'm so excited to go back in time and cuddle some babies who will grow up to become famous people."

"Babies?" Dana's nose scrunches up like it just got a whiff of bin juice.

"Oh. Sorry. Are we not going back to see scientists as babies?"

She laughs as she gets in the tuk-tuk. "I want to see this person at the height of their power. I want to see them right on the cusp of changing the world."

I click my seat belt and make sure the photobook is double secured. "Are you talking about the moment Dig-D revealed he had a tattoo of a sandal on his shoulder? Because I read online that when he posted the photo, the gasp of every Glow in the world caused a sonic boom."

"Not exactly." Dana shakes her head at me and reaches for the red button. She jabs at it a few times, but nothing happens. "I think the button is broken."

I lean forward to tap it gently and the tuk-tuk stutters to life.

"Hmm," she says. "Strange I couldn't do that. By the way, why did we come back to your house instead of back to that grassy place where we left your nana?"

The tuk-tuk trundles along aimlessly as I think this through. "Because Nana said you need to have a crystal-clear picture in your mind's eye of where you want to go, and I couldn't really picture that grassy place. Can you?"

"No," Dana says, "not really."

"Do you think that's a problem?" I ask, as I check the glovebox for more dried mango.

The tuk-tuk proceeds to loop slowly.

Dana bites her lip as she thinks this over, then says, "Nah. And if it is, we'll work it out later. Anyway, are you ready?" She grins at me then closes her eyes, "Tuk-tuk, take me to the place in my mind's eye."

The three dots on the dashboard flash and it says, "Sorry, I don't recognize your voice."

"Argh," Dana growls in frustration. "So annoying." She taps something into her phone then holds it in front of my face. "Can you picture this in your mind's eye?"

On the screen is a yellow building with tall windows and a set of stone steps leading up to a grand door.

"Where is this?" I ask.

"I want it to be a surprise," Dana answers.

How exciting. Dana's surprises are always the best, like the time she made me a life-size model of AZ8's Woojin from recycled yogurt pots.

"Come on, Skylar," she urges, "concentrate on the picture."

I focus in on the details of the image: the leafy trees, a bicycle leaning against railings, three ladies in long dresses and large hats. Then, Dana claps her hands excitedly and says, "Get ready to glow!"

10
GLOW UP

A few seconds later we touch down on the very same street I was picturing in my mind's eye. "Whoa," I say, "I can't believe that worked."

Dana jumps out onto the posh-looking treelined street and stares up at the building she showed me on her phone. "You did it, Skylar. Great job."

"Thanks," I grin.

Three fancy ladies wearing long dresses and big hats, which look like Easter bonnets, walk past the tuk-tuk, and give us curious looks.

"Come on," Dana says, "let's go inside now."

I step down from the tuk-tuk and consider my photobook on the back seat – it's pretty heavy to keep carrying around, plus I'm sure it'll be safe here, left unattended on a random street at a random point in history. I follow Dana past the cute bronze bicycle propped against the railings, up the stone steps and through the creaky grand doors. Together, we climb a narrow staircase, then take two lefts and a right along a crumbling corridor and pause in the doorway of a dingy room. There are light brown wooden cabinets and white tiled counters.

"Oh, it's a science lab," I say. "I should have guessed."

"You know me." Dana giggles as she heads towards a little desk and strokes it like it's a pet. "Whoa, so whoa."

An odd metallic smell mixes with something citrusy and fresh.

"Are you going to tell me *whose* science lab it is?" I ask.

Dana makes her little squealing noise and clutches her hands to her heart. "I'm so excited right now, I might pass out."

"Don't pass out. Just tell me." My eyes snag on some papers strewn across the desk. The writing, while impressively neat, isn't English. "Is this French?" I ask. "Are we in France?"

Dana knocks me out of the way to look at the papers. "These are her notes!" she cries.

"*Whose* notes?"

I am again pushed aside as Dana spots something over my shoulder. "The famous black lab coat!" She reaches out as if to touch the long dark garment hanging from a peg on the wall, then stops and puts a hand to her face. "I can't believe this. Pinch me," she instructs.

Bit of a weird request, but OK.

"Ouch!" She jumps away from me. "Why did you do that?"

"Because you told me to."

"It was a figure of speech, Skylar." She rubs her side. "We're really here, in the lab of one of the greatest brains the world has ever known. Here, within these walls" – Dana darts around the space and gently caresses each wall – "many game-changing discoveries were made, including work which would save injured soldiers during World War One. Work which would lead to fighting the most horrible diseases of our times. Work which would inspire generations!"

"Sounds like a lot of work to me."

"Work which would … which would…" Dana puts a hand over her mouth as if to stop herself from crying.

"Calm down," I tell her. "Breathe."

She takes a series of huge uneven breaths which turn into a weird sort of gasping sound when she catches sight of what's in the bin by the desk. "Orange peel!" she cries. "And it's still in one piece; that's how I peel oranges too."

While there's so much to admire about my bestie, I've always thought the fact she can remove the peel of an orange while keeping it in one piece is one of the most impressive. Though I'm not sure what that's got to do with the greatest brain the world has ever known…

"Are we going to actually meet this famous brain?" I ask.

"Meet her?! No, we can't." Dana gestures down to her Lilac Eyes T-shirt, jeans and bright pink high tops. "I'm not dressed for it. Plus, I wouldn't know what to say. I mean, would it be weird if I showed the sketch of the tattoo I plan to get of her face when I'm old enough?"

Tattoo? There's only one person I've ever heard Dana talk about getting a tattoo of… "Marie Curie?" I bark. "As in the Polish/French scientist?"

"The one, the only."

Is she serious? "Didn't Marie Curie die of causes linked to radioactive poisoning?" I ask, peering nervously around the room. "And isn't this where she and her husband discovered radium? In *this* radioactive laboratory?" As clean as the room is, all I can now picture is danger.

Dana does a double-take, as if she's never seen me before. "Whoa, Skylar. How do you know all this?"

"Because I listened to your podcast, *Dana Explains*

Science, and the first five episodes are you fangirling over Marie Curie."

"Aww," – she makes a heart shape with her fingers – "thanks for the support."

"You're welcome – it's a great podcast. However, are we not in *extreme danger* right now?"

Dana shakes her head. "I laugh in the face of danger! Muhahaha!"

I sigh. Everything is telling me to escape this room but I know how much Dana loves Marie Curie – she even has posters of the woman on her bedroom wall.

"I can't believe this is the same air she breathes," Dana says as she takes a deep breath. "It even smells smart."

Footsteps outside make us both freeze. I grab Dana and we duck behind the long black coat hanging from the hook. The tap, tap, tap of shoes enters the lab and I peek at a small woman with grey hair pulled back into a bun.

Marie Curie!

Beside me, Dana begins to recite the periodic table, something she only does in times of extreme nervousness. "Hydrogen, Helium, Lithium, Berylli—"

"Stop it," I hiss, taking another peek.

Curie sits at her desk, reaches into a pocket of her

long black dress and pulls out an orange, which she carefully peels.

"Does she speak English?" I whisper once we're safely back under the coat.

"Does the sun rise in the east?" Dana asks.

"I don't know. Does it?"

"It was a rhetorical question, Skylar – of course Madame Curie speaks English. The woman is a polyglot."

"A poly what now?"

"A polyglot: she speaks four languages, including English."

"Impressive. Why don't you get a selfie with her then we can time travel to somewhere cooler, like when AZ8 first played Wembley or, ooh, let's go back and see ourselves as babies. I bet you were extremely cute."

Dana rolls her eyes. "No, I want to stay here and continue to bask in her greatness."

"You want us to stare at her peeling fruit?" I ask, disappointed. "Isn't this a bit creepy?"

We both peer around again. Curie pops the whole fruit in her mouth and puts her little feet up on the desk.

"Whoa," Dana utters. "Fascinating."

Watching her eat is silly … plus I'm getting super-hot under this coat. It's time for Dana to meet her idol.

With a flourish, I pull the coat away from us and call out one of the five French words I know: "*Bonjour!*"

Curie jumps out of her seat, throwing the orange peel in the air in shock.

Dana drops into a curtsey. I don't know why she's doing this, as I don't remember anything on the podcast about Curie being royalty, but Dana knows better than me, so I copy, bowing low.

"*Bonjour,*" Curie says, her eyebrows cocked in question.

"Madame Curie, mother of modern physics." Dana's voice shakes like snake. "Please forgive us for interrupting your important work, your incredible work, your brilliant, awe-inspiring work, your..."

Dana seems to have short circuited, so I take over. "Hi. I'm Skylar and this is my bestie, Dana. She's a big fan of yours, huge. So, er, what ground-breaking developments are you working on today?"

"I'm not," Curie mumbles. "That's the problem. I'm having a *mauvais jour.*"

"Is that something you put in a baguette?" I ask.

She gives me a grave look, like the ones teachers do when I give a wrong answer, and then bursts out laughing. She cackles so hard orange juice splutters through her nose, which only makes her laugh even harder. I look at Dana for explanation, because I didn't think it was *that* funny, but Dana just shrugs.

"Baguette!" Curie hoots, as she calms herself down. "No, no, I meant I'm having a bad day. Sometimes, no matter what I do, I get so stuck I can't work it out." She reaches into her pocket and takes out another orange.

I nudge Dana. "Talk to her," I mutter.

"I can't."

Curie groans and starts garbling something in French. She sounds annoyed, and I think maybe we've outstayed our welcome.

"Are you..." Dana says, her voice small. "Are you OK, Madame? Is there anything we can do to help you?"

"It's the experiment," Curie says, gesturing to her notes. "I'm stuck on the conclusion."

We approach her desk. The notepad is open on a page of gobbledygook. I push out a long dramatic breath. "Looks tricky. Maybe you should ask someone in Year Ten."

Curie's blue eyes blink up at us hopefully. "Are you Year Ten?"

"Afraid not. We're Year Seven."

Dana's face has gone all weird. It's bright red, her eyes are shut and she's breathing heavily. She grabs me by the elbow and drags me back under the coat. "I know the answer," she says.

"You know, I always thought it was a common misconception that you're a genius but now I think I might have been wrong."

"I know it because it already exists," Dana says. "Because Madame Curie already worked it out and it's public record."

"So, tell her," I plead. "Put that tiny, stressed woman out of her misery."

"Tell me what?" Curie has crept up on us and is now under the coat too.

"That you need to learn about personal space." I flip the coat away, freeing us all.

Curie takes a step back. "Tell me!" she commands.

"We were just saying that—" I stop as Dana shakes her head at me. Then she makes a flapping motion which I can only assume is the mime for *fly* or *dance*. "Huh?" Then she screws up her face till it's the ugliest, creepiest thing possible. "What are you doing?" I ask through chuckles.

"Yes," Curie snaps, "what are you doing? I thought you had suggestions for my problem."

"No, no suggestions. I was just thinking about how powerful butterflies are," Dana says, eyeballing me.

Ahhh, I get it now. If she tells Curie what she knows, it will activate the butterfly effect. An idea hits me that will help Curie *and* give Dana some fangirling time with her idol. "Actually, I do have a suggestion: take a break. When I'm stuck with my homework, I leave it for a while. Go for a walk. Make some toast. Have a bath. Eat some toast while *in* the bath."

Curie's eyes light up. "A break. You're right. That's it, that's what I need." She plants big kisses on each of our foreheads.

"Wow!" I cry. "Less of the physical contact, please."

Curie grabs her black coat off the peg and starts out of the door. "Join me," she calls back.

I turn to Dana, who is glowing – thankfully, not literally glowing after that radioactive kiss. She grins widely and totters behind Curie. "I can't believe this is happening. Do you think Madame Curie likes me? I think she likes me."

Dana's joy is infectious, and I can't help but grin too, as I follow them both down the stairs and out onto the street.

"I'm going to take you both to the finest patisserie in all of Paris," Curie declares.

Patisserie? I picture all those delicious fancy French cakes. Now, that does sound enjoyable.

"*C'est incroyable!*" Curie hoots as she heads straight towards the tuk-tuk. "I haven't seen one of these in years."

Huh?

Curie kicks at the wheels with a tiny foot and chuckles. "Is this the model that takes the Flux-FSCH-55? I thought these were banned."

Again, *huh*?

My brain aches with confusion as I watch Curie inspect the tuk-tuk. "Do you know what this machine does?" I ask her.

"Why yes." She nods. "It's a food truck specialized in delivering delicious burritos."

"Yes." I giggle nervously. "Of course that's what it is. Why would it be anything more than that?" The skin on my left arm immediately blotches with the stress of outright lying. "Dana," I whisper, "I have a feeling something bad is about to happen."

"Really?" she whispers back. "Because I have a feeling something magnificent is about to happen."

"And I have a feeling," Curie whispers in quite a creepy voice, "that we're all about to have lots of fun in this tuk-tuk of yours."

I step away and shake my head. "No way, lady."

"What are you afraid of?" Curie asks. "Sure, the

authorities outlawed this model, but it's fine, as long as you don't go too far back." Curie slaps her own mouth closed. "I mean, don't go too fast."

And now, I'm *really* worried.

Curie peeks inside the tuk-tuk. "Ah, the dashboard has been updated. Where do you put the key?"

"It doesn't take one," Dana reveals. "It's a smart speaker. That means you—" I pinch Dana again. "Ouch," she moans. "Seriously, Skylar, stop hurting me."

"Yeah, Skylar," Curie says. "Stop hurting her. She was just about to tell me how a smart speaker works."

I desperately wave my hands at Dana and hope she understands that we cannot, under any circumstances, have any more historical heroes in the tuk-tuk.

Curie tuts, cocks her hip and looks directly at Dana. "Don't you want to come with me to eat pastries and talk science?"

Uh, oh. Pastries and science talk? Curie really knows her audience.

"Er, er, er..." Dana anxiously pulls at her own ears. "Yes— I mean no."

Curie steps closer to Dana. "I have some thoughts on quantum theory I'd love to share with a clever person like you over a *mille-feuille*. If only I knew how a smart speaker works..."

"You talk to it!" Dana blurts out.

Curie yelps and jumps in the front seat.

"What did you just do?" I ask Dana angrily.

"Did you hear what she called me? She thinks I'm clever. And *mille-feuilles* are unquestionably delicious."

"Dana, we can't let her drive the tuk-tuk."

"Why not?"

"Number one, I'm not sure I'm going to share her idea of fun. Number two, she's possibly radioactive. Number three, she's unusually short: I doubt she can reach the pedals—" The sound of a motor starting distracts me. "Hey!" I shout.

The tuk-tuk's lights flicker on and off and Curie leans out to yell, "Are you two coming?"

Dana doesn't wait. She jumps straight in the back seat and pats the space next to her for me to join.

The engine revs and I sense I don't have much choice. I step in and do up my seat belt. Curie hits the accelerator and we're off, cruising down tree-lined boulevards filled with pretty flower shops, alfresco diners and fabulously dressed French people.

Curie puts on the radio and mumbles along to the Portuguese pop songs, going "hmm laa laa" in a way which sounds even worse than when I try to sing an AZ8 Korean song.

My eyes snag on a clock face mounted on a lamppost, as it chimes 4 p.m. Already!

"Dana, I'm really confused about how time works."

She looks at me and says, "It's very simple. Time is the continued sequence of existence and—"

"No," I cut her off. "I'm confused about if time carries on when we're not there. For example, we left K-Mania at midday. Is it still midday there, or is it also now 4 p.m.?"

Dana raises her fist to the side of her head and mimes an explosion. "So confusing."

"Why are you confused?" I ask, slightly annoyed. "You're the smartest person I know. You should understand this."

Dana brushes her red hair from her face and grimaces. "For some reason, time differences are the one thing that I've never been able to get my head around. Last year, when I went to Greece with my family, the time difference was two hours, and my mind was completely blown the whole time."

From the front seat Curie hoots at our confusion. "You're funny little things."

"Her laugh is annoying," I grumble, still unclear on time differences.

"I love her laugh," Dana says. "It's like the tinkling of neurons falling from space."

The tuk-tuk slows in front of an elegant-looking patisserie, its window filled with flaky pastry and creamy cakey things. Finally! Maybe we *do* have time to stop for a quick snack before going back to get Nana and going forward to get Tut. I lick my lips as I spot a particularly delicious-looking choux bun, spilling with cream and drizzled with chocolate. I reach down to unclick my seat belt but the tuk-tuk moves off.

"Hang on," I say, glancing back at the choux bun in despair. "Why aren't we stopping?"

Curie giggles as the tuk-tuk speeds up and turns onto a busy street where we narrowly miss a cyclist balancing a large bunch of roses, a trolley piled with battered books and a man rolling wooden barrels into a restaurant.

"What is she doing?" I shriek.

"Don't worry, Skylar," Dana says, her voice bouncing with excitement. "We can trust Madame Curie. I'm sure she just wants to find the very best patisserie to take me to."

I study Curie in the rearview mirror and judging by the glint in her eyes and cheeky smirk on her face, I'm right to be suspicious. Suddenly, we take a tight corner and Curie lets out a hoot. "Oh, I forgot how much I loved driving one of these."

The tuk-tuk tips slightly to one side as Curie dodges two men in tall hats who are trying to cross the road. She yells something at them in French and they shake their cigars at her in anger. She sticks out her tongue and does a hasty U-turn.

"What is she doing?" I howl.

"I'm not sure," Dana replies. "She's a fantastic driver," Dana chuckles. "Did you see how she took that corner? Incredible."

We take another sharp turn and cut in front of a horse-drawn double decker bus. I look back as the coachman shouts what is possibly a French swearword at us. We are now driving so fast that I have to tuck my photobook into my dungarees for safety.

"I can't believe we're being fugitives with Madame Curie." Dana hoots with laughter. "This is the best moment of my life."

Curie takes her eyes off the road and asks in a crazed voice, "Who wants to go faster?"

"Not me," I say, while Dana squeals, "ME! ME! ME!"

I pull at Dana's T-shirt sleeve. "You need to stop being such a fangirl. Tell her to stop."

"I – I don't want to," Dana stutters.

"Why not?"

"Because I want her to like me."

"Yee-ha!" Curie hoots. "Oh, how I've missed *le voyage dans le temps*."

"What was that?" I mumble, confused at all the foreign language being thrown around.

Curie flips around, her eyes gleaming a little too wildly. "I said, I've missed time travel!" – and with that, she lifts her hands off the steering wheel and says, "Tuk-tuk, take me to the place in my mind's eye."

11

TWENTIETH-CENTURY FANGIRL

The tuk-tuk slams down and I slowly open my eyes. We're in a large field surrounded by trees trembling in the wind and heavy rain hammers against the roof. I shiver and cross my arms over myself. "It's so cold," I say through chattering teeth.

"Brrr," Dana says as she snuggles closer to me for warmth.

"1752," Curie announces over the clatter of the storm.

It's dark and grey but in the distance a round-bellied man and a younger guy in dapper clothes skip across the mulchy grass. They appear cheerful despite the fact they're getting absolutely soaked. The older-looking man is... I squint to ensure I'm seeing correctly and yes, he's flying a kite. In this weather!

"Who are those crazies?" I ask.

The men prance through the rain, singing, "La la la," while their kite gets whipped back and forth in the lashing gale. They stop to look up as a bolt of lightning flashes through the sky, then carry on, unbothered, as their shiny gold-buckled shoes and long white socks get splattered by muddy puddles.

I notice that a big metal key hangs off the end of the kite string.

"Is that Benjamin Franklin?" Dana asks.

Curie snaps her fingers. "Ah, you certainly know your scientists, don't you?"

"Are you kidding?" Dana does a big cheesy grin, the same one she did when AZ8 announced they were going carbon neutral at their concerts. "Franklin was not only a scientist, political philosopher, writer and inventor, he was also one of America's Founding Fathers. I know everything about him."

"Bravo!" Curie says. "You're very impressive."

"I've impressed Madame Curie," Dana says gleefully. "Feel my heart. It's beating exceptionally fast."

I pull my hand away from Dana's heart, which in my opinion is beating too fast to be healthy. "I'm freezing," I moan.

"Me too, but this is how Franklin thought he could

prove that lightning was electrical," Dana explains. "Definitely worth getting hypothermia for if you ask me."

Rain is now splattering us from all sides and I push my photobook deeper into my dungarees to keep it dry.

Curie cackles. "What next?"

"Well, if I'm honest," I say, "I'm quite interested in a warm bath and early bedtime."

"Boring," Curie says. "Booo to you!"

She's booing me? She's so rude. Then, worse than double Nobel Prize-winning Marie Curie booing my very sensible idea, is my best friend joining in. "Yeah, Skylar, booo!" Dana even adds a thumbs down. "We're having fun. We don't want to go home yet. Madame Curie, are there any other historical figures you would like to go back in time to meet?"

"Ooh, yes. Let me get my list," Curie says as she mimes unrolling a long scroll.

"You're such a joker!" Dana slaps her thigh, as if Curie has said the funniest thing ever.

"Isn't this bad for the butterfly effect?" I ask. "I don't think we should be pointing and laughing at people of the past."

Dana rolls her eyes at me. "You weren't saying that when you were singing 'Hot Feet' to baby Tae."

"It was a beautiful moment," I retort.

"Hey, Boffin," Curie calls, "come and sit up the front with me."

Dana is usually insulted when people call her boffin, though when Curie says it, she lights up. She climbs into the front seat and squeezes herself in next to Curie.

What happened to a quick peek at the past? This is turning into a full-on day trip. And neither of us has parental sign-off.

The rain stops and Curie lets the tuk-tuk glide over the dark fields while she chats with Dana. They're discussing wormholes, and not the kind made in the garden, but something specific to time travelling. I try to join in but I don't understand any of it.

Feeling a little left out, I look at my photobook instead. I dally in the *P* for petite-animal-related photoshoots section, because seeing AZ8 cuddle baby animals always cheers me up. I stop on an especially cute image of Garam gently cradling a gecko. Aww. Dana got me this one. I lift the book and lean forward. "Dana, remember when you won this photocard for me at the K-pop dress-up competition at Boom Busters Bubble Tea Cafe? That was such a fun afternoon, right?"

"What?" Curie shouts.

"It's nothing," Dana says.

What does she mean, *nothing*? "It's not *nothing*," I say. "We stood in line for three hours to be judged."

Dana whips around to face me. "Skylar," she bites, "Madame Curie isn't interested in hearing about a boy band, OK?"

Oh. That's mean. I lean back in my seat and close my photobook, realising sadly that my best friend is embarrassed by me.

"Anyway," Dana says, brightening as she turns back to her *new bestie*, "what's your theory on how gravity affects wormholes, because I'm obsessed with the idea that gravity's pull could cause them to collapse?"

They chatter away and I stare despondently at the endless passing fields. This weekend was supposed to be the best weekend ever. Yet I've ended up nearly three hundred years in the past with a mean radioactive scientist, and my best friend is ashamed of me. Not to mention the double disaster of an escaped Tut and misplaced Nana.

"Speaking of gravity," Curie says with a giggle, "you're going to love this next stop."

I know I'm *not* going to love it, but at least we're going somewhere.

The red button is pressed, Curie closes her eyes,

and as soon as she speaks the words she is *suspiciously* familiar with, the portal opens and we fly in.

We land in what appears to be someone's garden. There's a small manor house behind us and an orchard in front, which Curie proceeds to drive straight into. The sun is shining, the birds are singing and it smells of summer and cut grass.

"Ah, I love the fresh smell of nature," Dana says as she takes a deep inhale. "All these terpenes are so satisfying. This was a great choice, Madame."

Curie sticks her head out the side of the tuk-tuk and narrows her eyes. "Hmm. Where is he?" She drives slowly between neatly planted rows of trees which hang heavy with apples and pears.

"Who are we looking for?" I ask, but neither answer me. In fact, it's like they don't hear me at all.

Dana leans out of the tuk-tuk and stretches up to pluck an apple from a tree. "Here, Madame, I'm sure you could use a vitamin boost."

Curie grins at the red apple then takes a surprisingly colossal bite for such a tiny little lady.

I am *not* offered an apple, but it's fine. I don't want one anyway.

"How can you eat that?" I ask Dana as she wipes hers on the sleeve of her T-shirt.

"It's organic," she answers.

"Yeah, but it's not been washed. Disgusting."

Dana crunches away then says, "Supermarket fruit is covered in pesticide residues. And look, Madame Curie is eating it."

"Yes," I mumble under my breath, "but she's already dead."

We lurch forward as the tuk-tuk comes to an abrupt stop.

"A-ha," Curie says through a mouthful of juicy Braeburn, "there he is."

We follow her point to where a man sits under an especially large apple tree. He has long white hair, which curls fashionably over his shoulders, and judging from his outfit of shiny buckled shoes, long white socks and blue jacket with gold buttons, Peter Rabbit style, he's from the olden days.

"Is this Franklin again?" I ask.

Dana looks back at me. "You really don't know who that is?"

I study the figure, though, truthfully, I'm in no mood to play a guessing game. "I don't know. Mozart? Columbus? Santa Claus?"

Dana giggles, then stops when Curie tuts and says, "It's Isaac Newton. How could you not know?"

"Yeah, Skylar," Dana says as she sits up a little straighter and looks at Curie. "How could you not have guessed that? *Everyone* knows that, right Madame Curie?"

Curie nods.

"And this," Dana continues, slightly showing off, "is how he *claimed* to have discovered the law of gravity. Though many in the scientific community doubt his story."

"Yeah," Curie concurs. "Newton was a real exaggerator."

I've heard Dana talk about how incredible Issac Newton is too many times to let this slide. "I thought you said Newton was one of the cleverest people to ever walk the earth."

Dana swivels her head back to me. "I would never have said that."

"Yes, you did," I protest. "Those were your exact words."

Suddenly, Curie shouts, "BOO!"

Newton jumps. The poor guy bounces so high he knocks his head on a branch, and a heavy bunch of red apples comes tumbling down. "Ouch, ouch, ouchie!" he shouts as they fall, one smacking him right on the crown of his head. That's going to hurt tomorrow.

Curie laughs so hard her eyes water.

Newton rubs his head then catches sight of us. "What on earth—" he starts, but his words are sucked up by the sound of the tuk-tuk rumbling and Curie going, "Ha ha ha!"

We trundle on back through the garden the way we came, narrowly dodging fruit trees as the tuk-tuk picks up speed.

"Did you just heckle Isaac Newton?" Dana asks in a mixture of shock and admiration.

"I can't stand him." Curie laughs as she twists the steering wheel. "Such a show-off. Anyone else you want to see?"

Dana grips the side of her seat and even from back here I can see her knuckles are white, though she doesn't tell Curie to slow down. "I wouldn't say no to checking out Bibha Chowdhuri's laboratory."

"Who?" I call from the back.

"Or, ooh, I know, what about Charles Darwin?" Dana suggests excitedly. "Do you think it's possible to land the tuk-tuk on the HMS Beagle so we could check out his studies into evolution?"

I can't believe Dana was stressing about killing an insect yet now she's considering landing the tuk-tuk on a ship! I need to remind her of the stakes here.

"Excuse me," I interrupt. "We need to be getting back. Nana is going to be flipping out. Not to mention a certain iconic historical figure we've left alone at a certain K-pop convention."

"What's K-pop?" Curie asks. "That's the second time you've said it."

"It's nothing," I lie.

"Is it something from the future?" she asks, her eyes shining. "Is it something I discover?"

"Haven't you discovered enough?" I snap back.

"It is, isn't it?" Curie bounces excitedly in her seat. "That's why you're here, to make sure I discover K-pop."

"No," I protest. "That's not it at all."

She lifts her hands from the steering wheel, raises her arms in the air and declares, "Marie Curie, discoverer of radium, polonium and K-pop."

Honestly, I wasn't hugely bothered about the whole butterfly effect thing before, but now there's a possibility it could interfere with the greatest music genre on earth, I feel we have a problem.

"Boffin," Curie says, as she points at Dana's Karbon Neutral K-Pop Fan T-shirt, "is this K-pop? Side note, that's not how to spell carbon."

Dana looks conflicted. "Er, no. It's … nothing."

"And you in the back, that book you keep looking at, is *that* K-pop?"

"Nope. Not at all. Most certainly not." I hug my photobook close and try to think fast, which is tricky while being driven at speed by a madwoman. "K-pop is a type of … shoe."

"Shoe?" she asks, confused.

"Yeah," I say. "We left our friend at the shoe convention. That's it. Completely not relevant or interesting to you in any way." I hate lying, and as the words leave my mouth, the skin on my arms starts to break out into an itchy red rash.

"I don't believe you," Curie says, full of suspicion. "Let's time travel to the future, and I can find out for myself. Tuk-tuk, take me to the place in my mind's eye."

With a mighty flash, the portal appears ahead, shining bright. I hold my breath as the tuk-tuk lifts from the ground and … well … nothing happens. We're suspended midair, hovering at the entrance of the portal, as if someone's hit pause.

"Oh, how annoying," Curie moans as she slaps the steering wheel. "I don't know what the future looks like so I can't picture it," she explains. "This is why I got bored of time travel – it's too restrictive."

I sigh with relief, but my stress-free moment is cut

short when Curie turns to Dana and says, "Boffin, you know what the future looks like. Picture it and drive us some place fun."

"Me?" Dana says, "I can't. It doesn't recognize my voice."

"No problem," Curie says while gently patting Dana on the shoulder. "We can work together. You picture the future, and I use *my* voice."

Dana rubs her eyes with stress. "I'm not sure if it's a good idea."

"It's a terrible idea," I gasp. "Don't do it, Dana!"

"But you're sooo smart," Curie coos. "In fact, you remind me of myself at your age."

"Really?" Dana gazes at Curie with wide admiring eyes. "OK. Maybe I could try and picture—"

"No!" I yell. "Curie, we are not taking you to the future; now will you please stop being such an unruly side character."

She looks back at me and lets out a huge, affronted gasp. "I think you'll find I have main character energy."

"Stop arguing," Dana yells and then we're all yelling. Curie roars, "Think of the future," while I shriek, "Don't do it." This goes on and on until Dana's forehead creases and she begins to mumble, "Neon, Sodium, Magnesium, Aluminium—"

Not again. "Dana," I try to reason with her in my softest, calmest voice, "we're a team, remember?" I hear the words coming out of my mouth, though deep down I'm not sure if I have full belief in them: we haven't been on the same page for the whole of today. The whole weekend in fact. I can't take that chance.

I close my eyes and for once *I* do the thinking. I block everything I know about the future from my head and call to mind the past, history, days gone by, auld lang syne.

At first my mind automatically swings to all the bad stuff we learn about in school. Horrible wars, disastrous volcanic eruptions, no Internet.

"No, no, no. Bad thoughts, be gone." I shake my head and try again.

What else happened in the past? There's got to be something good and unthreatening. Then, I visualize what I originally wanted from this. The glorious greasy sensation of holding a whole roast chicken in my bare hands. Yes, that's it: the fantasy that got us into this mess in the first place.

I imagine myself at the head of a long wooden table, like the ones I've seen in school history textbooks, wearing a blingy, yet tasteful, crown. In the corner someone plays AZ8's "My Heart Goes Dry When You

Stop Loving Me" on a fiddle. There are tapestries on the wall, logs burning in the fire and I'm tearing an entire leg off a perfectly seasoned chicken and tucking in. It's such a clear image, except I stupidly can't pinpoint when in time it is. Tudor? Edwardian? Elizabethan? Shakespearean? Hang on, did Shakespeare really have his own time? What an overachiever.

"Tuk-tuk, take me to the place in my mind's eye," I say.

"What did you say back there?" Curie asks, as the tuk-tuk ambles forward.

"Shakespeare," I say, then no, no, no. "I mean, chicken. Tuk-tuk, take me to the place in my mind's eye. Take me to the chicken of Shakespearean times."

Is it working? Is the tuk-tuk actually speeding up?

I hear Curie say something in French which I ignore in favour of crying out the words, "Shakespeare" and "Chicken" over and over again like a crazed fan of poultry and boring plays. And then, *boom*!

12

FINGER LICKING!

The first thing I notice when we land, by a slow-flowing brown river, is that the sun is beginning to set, and the second thing I notice is the smell.

"Urgh!" I hold my nose to block the reek of rotting fish and fresh poop.

"It's the River Thames," Dana says, pointing at the little rowing boats heading to our side of the water. "We're back in London."

The riverside is buzzing, full of ye olde people in raggedy clothes milling about, laughing, shouting and generally having a great time despite the stench.

"London really stinks," I say.

Dana nods, "Back in the day, bad smells meant social progress."

"Better get used to the pong," Curie says as she taps a dial on the dashboard, "because we're not moving."

The tuk-tuk makes an odd wheezing sound, kind of like it's running out of breath. The wheeze turns to a whine, then a whistle, before it stops completely.

"It's done," Curie says.

"What?" I ask.

"The tuk-tuk," she says simply. "It's dead."

My eyebrows immediately sweat with distress. "No, it can't be." Nana is going to hit the roof. The tuk-tuk is her pride and joy, her livelihood, not to mention her secret time-travel machine. "It can't be dead. We need to bring it back to life. Because if we don't, we're—"

"Trapped," Curie says plainly.

Trapped?! No!

This whole time I've been worrying about where the tuk-tuk is going when really what I should've been worrying about is the tuk-tuk getting damaged and leaving us stranded in the past, Tut stranded in the future and Nana stranded in some undetermined era.

"Yes," Curie nods. "Trapped in..." She stops to look around. "I'd say 1610."

NOOO!

I'm a modern girl. I like central heating, sushi and on-demand television. I'm not cut out to spend the rest of my life in Tudor, Edwardian, Elizabethan or

Shakespearean times. And jeez, why were all these time periods so samey anyway?

"This is awful!" I howl. "This is the worst! I'm never going to see my family again. I'm never going to get to cuddle Kookie or get pizza delivered or enjoy high-speed Wi-Fi." I bring my hands to my face and blub into them.

The sound of amusement causes me to pause, and slowly I remove my hands to see Curie doubled over with laughter.

"It's not really broken," Dana, who is *also* laughing, says. "Madame Curie is messing with you. It needs a rest, that's all."

"Oh," I say, a little embarrassed – not because I missed the joke, more because I *was* the joke.

Curie tumbles down from the tuk-tuk, clutching her stomach as she chortles away, but Dana stops laughing to pat me on the shoulder.

"Don't worry," she says. "It was just a joke. Also, remember what your nana said, how the tuk-tuk needs to sleep overnight like a person? It also needs refuelling."

"So, let's find a petrol station," I try, keen to be helpful.

"It doesn't run on petrol," Dana says. "It runs on anaerobic digestion."

"Right. Yeah, I knew that." I step down too, careful to avoid the muddy riverbanks. "Let's go and find some anaerobic digestion then."

"You should have seen the look on your face," Curie says as she wipes tears from her eyes. "Hilarious."

She's really rubbing it in now. It's mean. I cross my arms.

"Oh, don't be such a softie," Curie says, finally picking up on the fact I am not enjoying the joke. "We're here now. This is what you asked for." She points over to a wooden stall perched on the side of the riverbank. It has a large torchlit sign above the counter painted with the words SFC Shakespearean Fried Chicken.

You've got to be kidding me!

Behind the counter two teenage girls in brown dresses and white bonnets stand picking their noses.

That's it. I've had enough – this day is terrible. "I want to go home," I whimper. Yet, as I'm saying this Curie is already marching away from the river, with Dana following closely behind. Reluctantly, I join them and together we make our way past barking dogs, beggars, bellringers and clucking escaped hens towards a large crowd gathered outside a peculiar, curved building.

"What is this place?" I ask.

"It's the Globe Theatre," Dana says.

"Doesn't look anything like a globe. Or a theatre."

The building is lit up with torches and surrounded by pungent-smelling people. A girl my age grabs me by the straps of my dungarees and yells, "I just want him to wave to me, then I can die happy!"

I gently unravel her hands. "Huh?"

"He's in there," she gushes excitedly, flashing a mouth full of black teeth.

"Do you have tickets for tonight?" two older men with grubby smiling faces ask. Their vibe is very excitable.

"I don't need tickets," Curie cackles, "I have unbound intelligence. Wait here, I'll get us in." She elbows her way into the crowd.

"What's playing?" I ask the men.

"*As You Like It*," one of them says. "I've already seen it twenty-seven times. And the last time I saw it, Rosalind looked right at me. Like this," he says, stepping forward so we're almost eyeball to eyeball.

"Great," I say as I take a step back and try to breathe through my mouth.

"Are you a fan too?" he asks.

"The biggest," I reply, and just as I'm about to clarify I'm not talking about whoever it is they're talking about,

Dana takes me by the sleeve. "Come on, Madame is calling us."

We snake through the crowd to where Curie stands chatting with a guard by the theatre gates. "Oh, Harold," she hoots, "always trying to charm me."

Dana bounces by my side. "Madame Curie knows everyone. She's the coolest."

"Whatever," I mumble as we follow the little scientist through the gates into the giant O-shaped building.

"You know, most people think the Globe is shaped as an O," Dana says, "but it's actually a twenty-sided polygon."

"Whoopee-do," I mutter.

We stand at the back of the empty theatre listening as Dana reels off fact after fact about the building. Then Curie gestures towards a tall man in a flamboyant burgundy outfit strutting towards us. "Here you go, Short Stuff," she says to me.

I stare blankly.

"It's the man you wanted to meet. William," Curie says, irritation in her voice.

"William who?"

"William *who*?" the man repeats as he puts the back of his hand to his forehead and gasps for air. "Oh, how my star has fallen. However, I must remember, it's not in the stars to hold our destiny, but in ourselves."

I lean in towards Dana and ask, "Is it William the Conqueror?"

"William Shakespeare," Curie says. "He's who you hijacked the tuk-tuk to see."

I think this over, and oh no. "I did, didn't I? I asked for chicken *and* Shakespeare." What a massive error. I was just so desperate to stop Curie from getting her mitts on the future *and* K-pop.

On hearing his name Shakespeare pirouettes and drops into a low bow. "Such a pleasure to meet a fan. I hear you won the competition."

"Yes, she did." Curie throws a wink my way. "The little one here won the annual search to find Shakespeare's biggest, most dedicated fan."

"Yes, I did," I lie. "That is true. That is the truth." I try my best not to scratch at the rash prickling up my arms. "I won, and now the prize is…"

Shakespeare does a short tap dance. "A tour of the legendary Globe Theatre by yours truly, plus tickets to tonight's sure-to-be-stunning performance of *As You Like It*, plus a one-night stay in the two-star inn next door including breakfast."

"Whoa." I try my best to sound excited. "That's great news."

"Plus plus plus…" Shakespeare giggles. "…my autograph." He rummages in his coat – because the Globe has no ceiling and is super chilly – and pulls out a long feather quill pen. "Hold on, let me get you one of my latest cards to sign."

"Boffin," Curie says, "come and help me find food waste for the tuk-tuk. We can have some deep and meaningful scientific conversations while doing it."

Dana smiles. "I'd be honoured."

I grab her by the arm. "What are you doing? You can't leave me here with him."

"Why not?"

I point to Shakespeare as he flicks through what looks like a ye olde photobook. "Stranger danger," I say.

"It's William Shakespeare." She laughs. "You'll be fine. He's not a stranger; everyone in the world knows him."

"He *is* a stranger and more troublingly, he's responsible for some of the most boring books I have ever had to read in my life. How am I going to convince him I'm his number one fan?"

"You only find the plays boring because you don't understand them. This is your chance to get a one-to-one lesson from the man himself."

"I don't want that." I stomp my foot. "Nobody wants that."

"And this is my chance to hang out with my idol," Dana says with a hand on her heart. "Can you imagine the wisdom Madame is capable of imparting on me. This is the kind of mentorship I could never have dreamed of. The kind of thing which could allow me to realize my ultimate ambition of winning a Nobel Prize before I'm thirty."

I thought Dana's ultimate ambition was to push through a nationwide ban on paper towels in all public toilets. "I think you're getting slightly carried away."

Her face falls. "I *am* allowed to do things without you."

"Oh." I recoil. While I knew Dana was enjoying showing off to her idol at my expense, I didn't realize she didn't want me there too. "Fine," I say, my voice a little high and unsure. "Go and talk science. I'll hang here with—" She doesn't even wait for me to finish my sentence before she scampers off to find Curie.

So, here I am, all alone in the past except for—

"There she is," Shakespeare says in what is very far from an indoor voice. "My number one fan in the whole wide world."

I try my best to grin at him. "That's me."

He holds up a small card, which kind of looks like a K-pop photocard. Though when I look closer, it's a painting of him with a full head of black hair and a youthful, smooth-skinned face. It's like how my dad refuses to update the photo of himself on social media as he wants everyone to think he's still twenty-two.

"Whoa, you look very different in this," I say. "Very … fresh faced."

My amusement must show because Shakespeare snatches the card and stares at it himself. "Yes, it is a slightly dated picture of me. Though I don't think I've changed much at all." He signs his name in big swishy writing and hands it back. "Are you ready to be dazzled by tonight's performance?" he bellows as he climbs the steps to the stage.

"I guess so."

"It really is a masterpiece!" he yells out at the hundreds of empty seats. "However, enough about *my* genius, tell me about yourself."

I follow his gaze to the invisible crowds. "Are you talking to me?" I ask, confused.

He nods down.

"Well, my name's Skylar Smith, I'm eleven years old and—"

"No, tell me how you first became my fan. What made you fall down the Shakespearean rabbit hole? Which play of mine is your favourite?"

My favourite play? He might as well have asked what's my favourite type of medieval torture. No, because at least I can name several of those, but his plays... Hmm, now let me think.

Ooh, I know. "*A Midsummer Night's Dream*."

"Truly a magnum opus!" he bellows.

"A what?"

"And who was your favourite character?"

"Errrr, errrr..." Think Skylar, think. "The main character, I guess?"

Shakespeare looks at me curiously and I feel guilty. Also, my rash is now getting very unsightly. I can't keep lying like this. "I'm sorry, I don't want to offend you, but I'm actually not a huge fan of your work."

"You joker, you!"

"No, I'm serious. I'm really not into your plays. Sorry."

His long face falls. "But I'm The Bard, the greatest playwright of the English language, the polymath of the pen."

"Yes, you are, but it doesn't mean everyone has to enjoy your stuff. I spent four weeks studying *A Midsummer Night's Dream* and I still don't have the foggiest idea what was going on." I try to recall what I learned during Mr Hardy's dreary English lessons. "There was a fairy and a magical child and— Urgh ... confusing."

"It's a very simple story actually," Shakespeare retorts, clearly offended. "Act one begins with Duke Theseus preparing for his marriage to Hippolyta, who of course is Queen of the—"

"Could you come down?" I ask as I rub the back of my neck. "I'm kind of short and it's hurting to keep looking up at you."

He jumps down from the stage, and we walk around the theatre while he chats away. Like, seriously, the whole time, without stop. No wonder he made so many plays because he's a man of many, many words.

As time ticks by, the actors, who are all boys, get ready for the show. They rush about backstage helping each other put on fancy costumes, giant wigs and flower crowns. There's a buzz building, and I must admit, it makes me excited to see the show. Maybe it won't be so bad after all...

"Say, are you coming to my party this evening?" Shakespeare asks as he tucks into a bowl of fishy snacks called periwinkles. He keeps trying to get me to try them, but I'd rather go hungry than slurp a seasnail from its shell.

"Not sure. What happens at a Shakespearean party anyway?" I ask.

"Oh, they're crazy cray cray. Cake and ale, jousting and poetry. I might even bust out a few lines of the old *Romeo and Juliet*, ha ha – everyone loves a classic." He glances down at himself. "I don't have a clue what to wear, though."

I consider Shakespeare, delighted to be able to help with something I'm good at. "Have you ever considered dyeing your hair pink? It would really bring out your jawline."

"Pink? I'm not sure I could pull it off with my complexion," he says with a stroke of his own cheek.

"I beg to differ." I get my phone out. "I have an app which shows you what you'd look like with different coloured hairdos and— Doh!" No Internet Connection. I totally forgot.

Shakespeare peers down and jabs at my screen. "That's an unusual little thing. What is it?"

I bet Shakespeare would love a smartphone, and I'm sure generations of people would thank me for making him less prolific, but no, I hide it away in my pocket. "Actually, I have something better." I take my photobook out of my dungarees and slam it on the table. "Here we have all the inspiration you need."

He makes lots of umming and ahhing noises as he flicks through pictures of AZ8. "These paintings are sensational. So lifelike! I must employ this artist for my next portrait."

"I think an obvious start would be getting rid of all that facial hair," I say. "Being smooth faced like a K-pop idol would take years off you."

"Ooh." He places a hand on his chin and strokes at the thin, spindly beard. "Beards are what distinguish the men from the boys, but … perhaps I should be the one to break with convention. So, you like doing makeovers, do you?"

"Makeover is my middle name," I reply.

"How unusual. Is that Norwegian?"

I go to *T* for photoshoots of AZ8 in traditional clothing. I switch my mouth side to side as I gaze at a shot of all eight members together, as they should be. I once saw an interview where AZ8 said they didn't even have each other's phone numbers as they already spent 365 days of the year together. Dana and I were amazed: the idea of being able to spend every waking moment with your bestie sounded like perfection. But now, with AZ8 taking a break, they probably never hang out anymore.

They might even have lost touch.

I picture Dana rushing off after Curie. Oh no. Is this what's going to happen to me as well?

I turn away from the photobook, because it hurts to be faced with what used to be. "Change," I say. "It ruins everything."

Shakespeare looks at me sympathetically, as if he understands exactly what I mean, and says, "If change be the food of love, play on."

Actually, no, he definitely didn't understand.

He pulls the photobook closer and gazes at the images with great interest, slowly appreciating the many fabulous AZ8 looks before stopping on one. "This is it," he announces in his big voice. He points to the photocard of AZ8 dressed as pirates. "This style is—" He stops and ducks his head into straightened arms as if catching a sneeze.

"What was that?" I ask.

"A dab," he says. "Back to the matter in hand, do you think this would suit me?"

I consider his current image – the lengthy face, the slightly thinning hair, the wispy beard – and, "Yes, I do. It would totally suit you. To the wardrobe department!"

An hour later and the gates are open, the theatre is filling and Shakespeare is backstage ready to unveil his new look to his company of actors.

"Are you ready?" He giggles from behind a purple velvet curtain.

"Yeah. Come on out," I urge.

More giggles. "No, but really, are you ready?"

"I'm ready, Shakespeare. Stop milking it."

His voice booms, "Introduce me, then."

"What?"

"I'm a star. Introduce me."

I sigh good-naturedly because it *has* been kind of fun hanging out with him while Dana is off talking science and collecting waste with Curie.

"OK," I announce, preparing my best movie trailer voice, "here goes. From the fields of Stratford-upon-Avon to the brightly lit stages of London comes a seventeenth-century renaissance man. You all know him, it's the number one playwriting poser himself, Williammmm Shakespeeeare." At this the curtain whips open with a cloud of dust.

Everyone claps when their eyes fall on a pink-haired Shakespeare with his new stylish orange pumpkin-shaped trousers and satin cape. He dramatically swishes the cape then throws it open to reveal a smart white shirt accessorized with ribbons and sashes. His face shimmers with crushed pearls, and a yellow tinted ruff around his neck makes his smile pop.

"You look amazing," I say.

He stands in front of the mirror and strikes a number

of poses. "Oh, Skylar Makeover Smith, how can I ever repay you?"

The bell chimes and Shakespeare grins. "Showtime!"

When I get to my seat, Dana and Curie aren't there yet. I can't believe they would miss seeing real-life Shakespeare performing, or that Dana would leave me alone for *this* long. I'm even more surprised that when the play starts, it's captivating. There's something about seeing the performance in real life, with all the magic and spectacle, which gives me goosebumps. People spring from trapdoors, fairies fly down from the stage roof and at one point there's a fire, which is a little scary considering the amount of straw around here, but it does add to the excitement.

There's also a great range of snacks on offer. I chow down a roast potato, a bag of plums and even try the fishy periwinkles, which are unexpectedly delicious. I eat so much that when the whole chickens are served, I must pass.

As act five begins – yes, there really are five acts and I'm enjoying them all – I take another look at the empty seats next to me.

Where are they? They're missing everything.

13

CHANGE

When Dana and Curie still haven't turned up by the end of the play, I begin to worry. Has something happened to them? I don't know a lot about Shakespearean England, but some of the people hanging around outside the theatre earlier certainly appeared dodgy.

Beginning to panic, I turn down Shakespeare's invite to his afterparty and rush over to the two-star inn next door. Hopefully they both just fell asleep and I'm worrying over nothing.

As I head towards our room, I swear I hear … Lilac Eyes? Is the song so catchy that I'm even hearing it in seventeenth-century England? I open the bedroom door and once my eyes adjust to the dim candlelight, I see Dana. Not being pushed around by olden-day criminals and not sleeping, but popping and locking to "Water" as it plays tinnily from her phone. Worse than that is Curie, who is right next to Dana, mimicking the dance while laughing and humming.

They left me on purpose – I can't work out whether to feel angry or upset.

"I love this!" Curie hoots.

Dana shimmies and yells up at the ceiling, "Me too. Having a Lilac Teer for a bestie is the best thing ever!"

My heart plummets. How could Dana say that? I'm supposed to be her bestie.

"Oh, there you are," Dana says. "Did we miss the play?"

"By about three hours," I mumble, trying not to cry. "Yes."

"Short Stuff, I was wondering where you disappeared to." Curie wipes the sweat from her brow and takes a breath. "I'm afraid all this dancing has tired me out. I'm off to bed. Thanks for such a fun day, Boffin. *Bonne nuit.*" At the door she stops to flick a finger heart at Dana, who returns it, and then they both smile at each other.

I can't even look at them anymore, it hurts too much.

Once Curie leaves, Dana sighs happily. "What a great day," she says.

"Well, you and Marie Curie seem to be getting on like a box of hair dye and a K-pop idol," I comment sarcastically.

"What's that supposed to mean?" Dana asks.

But I'm too full of mixed feelings to say anything else right now.

We go about our bedtime routines, which are severely limited as we didn't bring our overnight bags. My anger causes me to slam things around and my sadness makes my bones heavy as I finally climb into the creaky wooden bed.

Dana's phone is on the side table, and it lights up to alert her it's running out of power. My heart sinks even further as I notice her home screen is no longer the photo of us posing with the life-size Woojin made of recycled yogurt pots. No, it's now some generic photo of Lilac Eyes, their four perfectly-made-up faces grinning, pouting and, admittedly, looking remarkably cute and cool.

"Why did you change your home screen?" I ask as Dana jumps in the bed next to me.

She scrunches her nose up. "Oh, I was getting bored of it."

Is she serious? "You're bored of me?"

"I never said that."

"You didn't need to." I pull the covers up around my chin and roll away from her. She's bored of me! That's it! It hurts so much I have to grit my teeth and squeeze my eyes to stop myself from crying.

"Skylar, why are you so upset?"

I sit up in the bed and push the itchy covers away from my face. "How do you expect me to feel? All weekend you've been letting me know you're bored of AZ8, and now you're bored of me."

"I never said that," she repeats. "But Skylar, I'm allowed to like other things, other bands, other people. Just because I change, it doesn't mean we're not friends anymore."

There it is again, stupid change messing everything up.

"Also," Dana says, "change is good for our cognitive health."

"I'm tired," I yell suddenly, making Dana flinch. It doesn't feel good. I put my hands over my eyes and when I'm sure I won't shout again, I say, "I'm tired and I don't want to talk about cognitive health right now."

"Change is good for us," Dana says. "But if you can't be friends with a Lilac Teer, then maybe I'm the one who needs to move on."

"Fine," I shout, my voice wobbling with emotion.

"Yeah, it is fine," she shouts back.

Don't cry, I tell myself, *Don't cry.* I blow out the candle and hide myself back under the covers.

Despite the relaxing rhythmic sound of the lute

from the party in the theatre next door, sleep doesn't come. I'm worried. And if I'm honest, I've been worried for weeks. At first, I thought it was because everything and everyone else was changing – running triathlons, working all the time and going on "breaks". But now I realize I'm worried because I'm *not* changing. I'm the same boring old Skylar I've always been and that's it. That's the problem.

No wonder Dana doesn't want to be my bestie anymore, and my parents don't want to spend their weekends doing normal parental things with me anymore. No wonder Nana didn't tell me the truth about the tuk-tuk. It's because … I'm boring.

The next morning, I'm the first one up. I head to the dining room where a friendly-looking maid greets me. "What would you like for breakfast, dear?"

"A bowl of your finest cereal, please." Because even though I'm boring and had the single worst night's sleep of my life, I'm still hungry.

She rubs her hands together. "Lovely, I'll nip out to the cows for the milk then."

Er. What? "Actually, it's OK. Do you have any periwinkles left?"

The maid smiles as she fetches a bowl of the

delicious salty snacks for me.

Shakespeare stumbles in. He's wearing big dark sunglasses, and his hair is a mess. "Why is the daytime so bright?" he groans.

"Fun party?" I ask.

"The very best. I was up till 4 a.m. I hope no one painted me last night. I was jousting like a madman."

It's here I realize two things: one, I'm not 100 per cent sure what jousting entails; and two, the complete removal of facial hair was perhaps a little extreme for someone with a jaw as long as his.

"Oh, that last poetry reading was a mistake," he says. "I'm so tired. And I'm going back to Stratford-upon-Avon later – it's my granddaughter's sports day tomorrow."

"Cool. Are you getting the train?" I ask.

"What is *train*?" he asks curiously.

Oops! "Nothing. Ignore me." I shove a few periwinkles in my mouth to stop myself from talking.

Shakespeare picks up a silver spoon, checks his reflection in it and grins. "This has been good for me." He waves a hand over his face. "This new look. The fans are going to go wild."

"You don't think it's too much change at once?" I ask, observing the hasty hair dye job.

"No, not at all. The more dramatic the change, the better."

I blow a raspberry. "Personally, I think change is overrated. Things are much better when they stay the same. When your mum works her normal job, rather than going away every weekend. When your dad is happy to simply think about running, rather than doing it. When your nana doesn't change up her whole, entire routine. And when boy bands stay together and make music and tour indefinitely, for ever, without a break and … and … and…" I stop to grab another mouth-stuffing periwinkle.

Shakespeare takes off his sunglasses and stares at me for an uncomfortable amount of time.

"What?" I ask, embarrassed at the way my voice cracks. "Why are you glaring at me? Do I have an eye bogey or something?"

"Oh, Skylar," he sighs. "No, time, thou shalt not boast that I do change."

I'm way too emosh to try to work out what this means. "Huh?"

"People change, Skylar. They move on. But the band that seems to tie their friendship together will be the very strangler of their amity."

"Really, Shakespeare, I'm working on like four

hours' sleep here – please speak plain English to me."

He stands, climbs on his chair and booms, "Imagine, if you will, a world without change. A world where things stayed the same today and for ever."

I try to imagine a world stuck in Shakespearean times, with snails for breakfast, no Internet and poetry readings as a form of entertainment. It turns my stomach.

"Not great," he says to me, "is it?"

"No, I guess not."

"Everything must change. To grow. To move on." He jumps down from the chair and points at me. "You're growing and moving on, too."

"I'm not," I moan. "That's the problem. I'm the same. It's the whole world around me that keeps changing."

"You've changed in the few hours you've been here."

I shake my head. "No, I haven't."

"Yesterday, you hated theatre. You sank at the thought of watching a play, and now you positively love it."

I raise a palm. "Well, I wouldn't go *that* far."

"Also, your eating habits: I recall you first turning your nose up at periwinkles, yet you've eaten a family-sized portion of them since I came in."

I gaze at the empty bowl in surprise. Is Shakespeare

right? Have I, in less than twenty-four hours, changed into a theatre-appreciating snail eater? And if so, is this a good change?

Shakespeare sits back down, then Curie and Dana come in, chatting and joking with each other. Dana is wearing Curie's long black lab coat over her T-shirt and jeans. Talk about extreme fangirling! She catches me looking and whooshes it around. "You like?"

"No," I say, as I turn myself away from her. I can't believe that after last night, Dana still chose to get up and hang out with Curie rather than have breakfast with me.

The maid hands Curie a tall glass of milk which she gulps downs. "Yum, still warm," she says, wiping her milk moustache. "Let's go."

Shakespeare walks us back to the riverside, stopping to sign autographs for a few adoring fans who have spent the whole night camping outside the theatre to catch a glimpse of him.

As I get in the back of the tuk-tuk, I take off one of my long dangly earrings: it's the same one Garam wore in the video for "The Moon Shines in Your Face". Except, it's not quite the same because his cost the same as a car and mine is from a website called jewelsremadecheaply. com which Nana discovered.

"Here." I hand the earring to Shakespeare. "You can wear this when you're after some extra swag."

"Thank you," he gushes. "I'm going to make this the hottest accessory this side of the century."

I get in the back seat and watch as Dana approaches. She stares at the empty space next to me but doesn't make a move.

"Come up front," Curie calls at her.

And with that, I spread out across the back seat and Dana goes to the front.

I try not to take it personally.

"Interesting choice of transport you have here," Shakespeare says while eyeing up the tuk-tuk.

"Don't you know it, mister." Curie presses the red button and the tuk-tuk splutters to life.

"Skylar," Shakespeare cries, "aren't you forgetting something?"

The tuk-tuk is already jerking forward a little, as it struggles to move off the muddy banks of the river.

"What is it?" I ask as he quickens his step alongside us. "Is it more periwinkles, because your maid already gave me a doggy bag."

"No, it's your book of fabulously dressed young men."

I gasp. I can't believe I almost left my photobook here. "Stop the tuk-tuk!"

Curie cuts the engine while Shakespeare turns and runs back towards the inn. The three of us sit in an awkward silence while we wait.

"Thank you so much," I tell him when he returns, slightly flushed and out of breath. "I appreciate it. In fact, I appreciate you and your plays."

Curie must have hit the red button again as the tuk-tuk chokes to life and the engine hums under us.

"*Au revoir*," Curie calls as she finally gets it out of the mud.

"*Adieu*," Shakespeare says back.

"*La revedere*," Dana says.

"Bye!" I yell.

"Who's choosing the next adventure?" Curie asks as we pick up speed.

"No more adventures," I say. "It's Sunday morning. We need to work out how to put things right." My mind boggles each time I think of all the history-causing chaos we've set in motion. Helping Tut escape ancient Egypt, then setting him free at a K-pop convention to sing about feta cheese. Taking Marie Curie to old London in search of chicken and Shakespeare. Not to mention the fact we've left Nana in … well, I don't even know where or when. "Seriously," I say to Curie, "you need to go back to France, and we need to sort things out."

"Do you hear that sound?" Curie asks me.

"No, what sound?"

"The sound of me falling asleep." She cackles. "Your ideas are so dull." At this, Curie nudges Dana in the arm, but Dana lowers her eyes to her lap and doesn't laugh.

The tuk-tuk continues to trundle along the banks of ye olde River Thames before Curie, in a very annoyed voice says, "Come on Boffin, where do you want to go?"

Dana shrugs her shoulders, and an uneasy atmosphere fills the tuk-tuk. Curie casts a look back at me and then a look at Dana before huffing. "This is no fun."

I cross my arms and stare out at the river, watching the bobbing of broken carts, glass bottles and cabbages. But it's not a big enough distraction and soon my eyes fill with tears.

Curie slams the steering wheel. "Can't you think of something you both agree on?"

Dana and I look at each other and I wipe my eyes on the shoulder of my T-shirt. I hate this. Time travelling is meant to be fun, not tearful. "We don't agree on anything," I say. "We have opposing views."

"Yeah," Dana says, her voice also shaky, "I like a girl group and she likes a boy band."

"I like sugar snap peas," I blub, "and she likes mushy peas, which shouldn't even be considered a real food."

Dana, who is also now crying, wipes her eyes on the black lab coat. "I like new things and she just wants to like the same, old thing for ever and ever and—"

"That's unfair," I bawl, "AZ8 aren't an old thing."

"*Bonté divine!*" Curie shouts. "I'm not asking you to write a thesis on radioactive substances, I'm simply asking you to find one thing you both like. I can't go back to Paris and leave you two with all this tension. It'll give me indigestion." Curie grunts then says, "Perhaps there's a memorable moment in time you shared? What do you enjoy doing together?"

I picture us in the canteen at school, crouched over my phone as we watch an AZ8 dance practice video. Dana laughing as I mimic the moves, taking a spin too sharply and falling into the salad bar. I picture us sitting on my bed, playing AZ8's greatest hits while singing at the top of our lungs, Dana impressing me with how quickly she picks up the Korean lyrics. And finally, I picture us on our last school trip to the world-famous British Museum. We didn't bother looking at any of the priceless artefacts because Garam went live on the Live-Right-Now app and we had to sneak away to watch him talk about scented candles for 45 minutes.

So much of our friendship is wrapped up in AZ8 and being Glows, but that's not all we are.

"Well, then?" asks Curie, who in a blatant disregard for road safety, has taken both hands off the wheel to peel an orange. I don't know where she keeps getting all this fresh fruit from! "I'm waiting?" she prompts as she balls up the single long piece of peel.

I look at the back of Dana's dipped head and sloped shoulders. She turns to me and, as we stare into each other's eyes, the portal appears ahead of us.

"You know what I'm thinking of?" Dana asks.

And because, deep down, I know she's still my bestie, I nod my head and say, "Yes. I do." Then I close my eyes and say, "Tuk-tuk, take me to the place in my mind's eye."

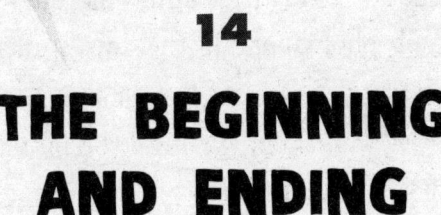

14
THE BEGINNING AND ENDING

We land in the garden of our secondary school, Saint Margaret's Academy. Well, it's called a garden, but the only thing that grows on this patch of concrete is fear of the Year Ten bullies who usually dominate this space.

"You pictured school?" Curie asks, sending a confused look my way.

"Yes," I admit. "Though I don't know why. It just popped into my head."

"Mine too," Dana says from the front seat.

Without another word, we all step out of the tuk-tuk and walk through the open double doors to the main corridor, silent apart from the distant murmur of voices from a classroom. Curie follows and stops by a huge display board with a banner above which reads *Hard Work Conquers All*.

"*Fantastique!*" she proclaims as she gazes at hundreds of photos of all the top students, each one the best or quickest or first at doing something. "All these hard-working high achievers. It gives me goosebumps."

"I hate it," I say. "When we first started at Saint Margaret's, only the smartest of the smart got praised. I'm so glad the school isn't like this anymore." Then it hits me – we're not in the present day. "This is Saint Margaret's back in September, back when it was a miserable, soul-destroying place to be."

Dana joins us at the display. "You're right, Skylar. Why are we here?"

I gasp. "More importantly, what happens if we bump into ourselves?"

Dana shakes her head. "That would never happen because that would be too weird to— Arggh!" She pushes me away from the display and round a corner as someone skips down the corridor. "It's you, it's you!" she squeaks while pointing a trembling finger.

I take a nervous peek. Skipping down the hallway, in the original Saint Margaret's uniform of a tan pleated skirt, boxy brown blazer, mucus-coloured shirt and mustard socks, is me! Me – completely oblivious to the fact that future me is standing a few metres away.

It's surreal and … "I can't believe I'm that short in real life!"

"Told you," Curie cackles.

"I'm almost primary-school sized—"

"Shh!" Dana puts a hand over my mouth. "Do you really want your past self to hear your future self making comments about how vertically challenged you are?"

I remove her hand once I'm sure I'm calm. "I remember this," I whisper. "I asked to leave class to use the toilet, but really, I just wanted to have a little stroll." I smile as I realize that we're about to see one of the most beautiful moments of our lives replayed. "Keep watching. Now I'm going to have a sneaky Hubba Bubba and check my phone for any important AZ8 updates."

We watch as Skylar of the past chucks three bubble gums in her mouth then breaks the strict no mobile phones rule. I know exactly what happens next and it warms my heart more than seeing photos of Dig-D in a pink beanie hat.

"Now, you're also going to come out of class," I tell Dana.

"No," she whispers back. "That can't be right: I never make excuses to get out of class. I love class. Being in class is among my favourite 25 hours in the week and— Oh!" She stops and points an even tremblier finger at the past version of herself. Also, in full original Saint Margaret's uniform and a hall pass lanyard around her neck. "Oh right, I was out of class on official business. I look so youthful."

Curie sticks her small head in between our shoulders and murmurs, "The world has existed for 4.5 billion years, yet you two chose to go back a few months to look at yourselves?"

"Dana, this is the first time we ever spoke, right after we flicked Korean finger hearts at each other in the assembly hall."

Past me has a Woojin keyring on her rucksack, as Woojin used to be my bias. And past Dana has a Garam keyring, as he used to be her bias. We spot each other's keyrings and enormous, matching grins spread across our faces.

"So," past me says, "you're a Glow?"

Past Dana nods. "Yeah. You?"

"Yeah." Past me nods back.

Past Dana says, "Wanna be besties?"

Past me nods and then another, "Yeah."

From behind us, Curie stifles a laugh.

I give her my most irritated face. "Why are you

sniggering through such a profound moment in our lives?"

"Was this really your first conversation?" she asks. "Hardly riveting."

The past versions of us are now discussing many an important topic such as if we think Haru's lip piercing is real and how much we appreciate Dig-C's commitment to hitting a high note while holding a one-arm handstand. We chat and chat as we walk off towards the bathrooms, our happy voices fading down the corridor.

"That was it," I say, emotion bubbling up through my belly. "The moment we became besties."

There's a sniffling next to me and when I turn to Dana, a tiny, glittery tear runs down her face. "I want to be your bestie for ever," she says.

"Me too," I agree, feeling overwhelmingly emosh and tearful. "I want to be your bestie till we're old and wrinkly, like Marie Curie."

Curie tuts and crosses her arms.

"I want to be your bestie as much as I want the Tapanuli orangutan to come off the WWF's threat of extinction list," Dana says.

"I want to be your bestie till AZ8 end this ridiculous *break* and do a huge comeback where we can turn around to everyone who said boy bands never reform and say, *Ha! Told you so*."

"Me, too!" Dana squeals, and this makes me the happiest of all. "And I want to be your bestie until … until… I've run out of things, but I really want to be your bestie for ever."

Then we hug, cuddle and squeeze. It's a beautiful moment until the sharp smell of orange hits us as Curie wraps her arms around our huddle. I yelp and step away. "Let's *imagine* the cuddle," I say, because despite how annoying she is, I don't want to hurt her feelings.

Ah, it feels good to have my bestie back. I've missed her so much. "Now we're friends again, we should get matching AZ8 glitter tattoos at K-Mania to celebrate."

Dana squeals with excitement. "Awesome idea. I'm also thinking, super-sized Korean mozzarella corn dog to share."

My mouth waters at the thought. "Ooh yes, and a coconut bubble tea."

"Yes, and a— Hang on…" Dana's smile suddenly melts off her face. "We're getting carried away. Before all this, there are some very big things we need to sort out."

"Yeah," I agree, "we all need a shower and a fresh pair of socks."

"No." Dana shakes her head. "I meant more the need to find your nana, repatriate King Tut and get out of here. Can you imagine the catastrophic butterfly effect of past us running into future us?" She laughs.

I do a little unsure laugh too, because even trying to understand what that would look like and what it would mean makes my eyeballs hurt.

"How impressive!" Curie says. We look behind us, only she's no longer with us. In fact, she's halfway down the corridor talking to Mr Keen.

Dana fake cries. "Oh no, anyone but him." Dana idolizes all teachers, who she refers to as the fount of knowledge – all teachers *except* for Mr Keen who we once caught googling *Are primary school and secondary school different things?*.

"Is this what you meant by more catastrophic butterfly effect stuff?" I ask Dana.

"This is exactly what I meant."

Curie does her over-the-top laugh and Mr Keen chuckles along. Then, as we get closer, we hear him say, "I'm also something of an inventor. I came up with the idea of the Internet before anyone else."

"The internet?" Curie says as she pulls a pencil from her grey bun of hair. "That sounds so interesting, tell me more."

Dana lifts the hem of the long black coat in front of her face. "Mr Keen mustn't see us," she whispers.

"Why not?" I ask, as I too get under the coat, which smells like Curie's lab and oranges. "If this is the first day of school, he won't know us yet."

"No, but what happens when we have our first Computing class with him and he says, "Hey, aren't you the girls that were in the hallway with that twentieth century chemist the other day?"

"Ah, I see your point."

"Can I get your email address?" Mr Keen says, to which Curie answers, "Sure, it's 115 Rue de Paris—"

"Madame!" Dana shouts in a funny, obscured voice. "Come over here quickly, someone is giving away a free box of pipettes and test tubes."

As Curie follows us back down the corridor to the garden, Mr Keen calls, "Hey, is your surname spelt with a curly C or a kicking K?"

We push through the double doors and close them tightly behind us before getting back into the tuk-tuk. As the engine warms up, I give Dana a high five.

"Hold on," Dana says as she gets out her phone. "While we have the Internet, I should double check… Oh dear."

Curie and I watch as Dana reads something on

her phone, which is something terrible judging by the expression on her face. "What?" I ask, my belly full of bouncy balls.

She blows out a stressed breath. "No. No. No. I was searching for information on Tut. There's nothing."

I picture a giant timeline of the last two days... The first day of school was the third of September; K-Mania isn't until the fourth of April the following year. Of course there are no updates on Tut. Why is she getting stressed about it? "Dana, there are no updates about Tut at K-Mania because it hasn't happened yet."

Dana bites her bottom lip. "No, Skylar, it's worse than that. No one's posted anything about Tut. At all. Ever!"

"What?" I too am starting to panic. I look at her screen and it is indeed a no, no, no situation. Dana's got a search engine open and is repeatedly typing in the words King Tutankhamun and getting *zero* search results.

"Maybe you're spelling his name wrong," I offer, "because it does have like eleven letters and is—"

"Skylar, I know how to spell Tutankhamun Nebkheperure, OK? Nope, he's not online. Do you know what this means?"

"That King Tut needs to work harder on building his online brand?"

"No," she says. "King Tut doesn't exist."

How can he not exist? We literally saw him yesterday. I am so thoroughly confused.

"We've messed up," Dana whines. "Because of us, King Tut disappeared way back in 1331BC, which means he never got to rule for long, which means he never got the big fancy king-style tomb, which means there was never anything for the Egyptologists to discover in 1922, which means—"

"For the love of Garam's future best actor Oscar nomination, cut to the chase already," I demand.

"Which means," Dana shouts, while looking gravely serious, "we've basically wiped out an entire strand of world history!"

15

REWIND, FAST FORWARD, REWIND, FAST FORWARD

While Dana and I are processing this nightmare, Curie guides the tuk-tuk through the portal. When we land, we're back outside her building in Paris.

Dana looks worried. "Why are we here?"

Curie hops down and smiles. "Ah, I'm so glad to be home."

"Don't you want to help us sort out all the problems we've caused?" Dana asks.

Curie wrinkles her forehead as if in thought, then says, "Not really, no." She lifts her little arms in the air and takes a long stretch. "The good news is, I've figured out the answer to the problem *I* was stuck on earlier."

"Good for you," I say, glad she's back on track.

"Plus," Curie says with a waggle of her finger, "I have *boeuf bourguignon* with my daughters on Sundays." And with that, she walks off.

"Hold on," Dana calls, disappointment obvious in her voice. "Is that it?"

Curie turns and asks blankly, "What do you mean?"

"Two random girls turn up at your lab, you spend the weekend time travelling with them and then you just say bye and walk off like it was nothing out of the ordinary?"

Curie's face is unreadable as she looks from me to Dana and then to the tuk-tuk. Finally, she shrugs. "I live an extraordinary life. Exceptional things happen to me all the time. *Au revoir!*" She throws us a small wave and carries on.

We watch her go, then I turn to Dana and we both burst out laughing. "What just happened?" I ask.

"I have no idea!" she giggles. "But I do know, I'd love for you to come and sit up front with me."

I tuck my photobook under the seat belt and jump into the driving seat, flicking away all the discarded orange peel. "Right, let's find Nana."

"Actually," Dana says with a thoughtful stroke of her chin, "I think the Tut situation is more pressing.

Because effectively, we've ceased his existence, whereas with your nana, all we've done is left her chatting to an old friend somewhere."

Hmm. Dana makes a solid point. "Cool, so let's get Tut first so we can put him back in the past, where he can go on to live and then die in a tragic and untimely manner."

Dana snaps her fingers. "You got it."

I take one last look around the fancy streets of Paris and say, "You know, I'm kind of upset we never made it to a French patisserie."

"Me too," Dana agrees. "I've always wanted to try one of those gigantic croissants."

I hit the red button and wait for the dashboard to light up. "I've also always wanted to try real *boeuf bourguignon*, *coq au vin* and even *cuisses de grenouille*."

Dana wide-eyes me. "How do you know so much about French cuisine?"

"Nana taught me," I say sadly, because I miss her. "She loves French food." As the tuk-tuk moves slowly along the same streets we wheeled through yesterday, I fantasize about one day coming back to France with Nana. "Ah, France," I sigh. "The sights, the sounds, the smells."

Dana nudges me in the side. "Skylar, stop thinking

about French things. Your mind needs to be on England."

I shake my French thoughts away. "Yes, right. England. Rain and castles." The pace picks up and I close my eyes.

"The land of kings and queens," Dana says helpfully.

"Yes, and crowns and banquets and whole chickens." I peek to look at Dana as she laughs before adding, "Georgians, Stuarts."

"Tudors," I say. Thinking of England is easy. I close my eyes once more and whisper into the dashboard. "Tuk-tuk, take me to the place in my mind's eye."

We quickly gather speed as we near the end of the street, taking a sharp left and a soft right, and then the portal appears, and then – *kablam*!

We land in the back of a large hall, with high ceilings decorated with carved wooden heads. Creepy. In front of us are rows and rows of people, many of whom are wearing fancy gold crowns, the kind I aspire to own. A fiddle plays a chirpy tune and the smell of roast chicken hangs in the air. My stomach rumbles. Periwinkles may be delicious, but they're certainly not enough fuel till lunchtime.

"Shh," Dana says in the direction of my belly.

I cross my arms over my stomach, hoping none of

the people sitting in the pews heard.

"I think we're in Tudor times," Dana whispers. "How annoying. We're back in England, but it's not the present day."

I grumble. "This is all my fault. I was thinking of kings and queens."

"Me too. Don't worry, we can fix this. We just need to—"

Suddenly, loud, stirring music begins, and everyone turns to the back of the hall. We quickly duck down.

"Do you think anyone saw us?" I whisper. Though of course everyone saw us!

Dana gasps. "The music. You know what this is?"

"No, but I love playing guess the tune. Give me a second." I perk up my ears, keen to win the game.

Dum dum dee dum! Dum dum dee dum!

Ooh, I know it. I know it.

Here comes the bride. All dressed in white.

"Wedding music," I say. "I wonder whose happy day it is." We dare to peek over the dashboard and there at the bottom of the aisle, standing proudly as if he didn't do some really horrible stuff, is Henry VIII.

"Urgh," Dana says. "Henry VIII is my least favourite royal of all time. Why couldn't he have let a girl be his heir? So mean."

"Yeah, mean and stupid. Who is he marrying here?"

We look around the hall for clues. The walls are covered with brightly coloured tapestries and the sun streams through the stained-glass windows, casting rainbows across the aisles. It's so pretty and would make a great backdrop for a selfie. I spot a hand-painted sign which reads:

The marriage of King Henry Tudor VIII and Catherine Howard.
Please place all gifts below.

"Didn't he marry like six women? I can't believe he expected gifts every time," I say, a little more than mildly outraged. "He must have ended up with a lot of air fryers. Catherine Howard. Which one was she?"

Dana scratches her head. "I think she was the fifth…"

I'm pretty sure something bad happened to her. I try to remember the rhyme from History class. Dana is evidently doing the same as we both start humming while counting wives on our fingers.

"*Divorced, beheaded and died,*" we sing. "Then, *divorced, beheaded, survived.* BEHEADED! NO!"

"We can't let her go through with this wedding," Dana says.

"We also said we would stop changing history."

Conflict flashes across Dana's face. On the one hand I know she wants to save Catherine Howard, but on the other hand there's a small historical butterfly saying *Dana, please don't crush me!*

"Skylar," she pleads, "I don't know what to do."

"Just do the right thing. I'll support you."

Dana leans out of the tuk-tuk and shouts, "Catherine, don't do it!"

I lean out of the other side and join in with the hollering. "Run away, Catherine! Run as fast as your little Tudor legs will take you!"

The wedding guests gasp, they stand up and protest, some jeer, others shout and one woman in the front row cheers us and starts flossing.

"Run!" Dana shouts again.

"Shush those children," King Henry booms at a group of scary looking, yet also very fabulously dressed, guards.

"The Yeoman of the Guard," Dana shouts.

"I don't know what that is, but I'm loving their red and gold outfits," I comment. Though I do not love the way they are marching towards us, with their swords drawn. I slam on the red button and we start to move, right through the middle of the hall. Wedding guests gulp, squeal and jump away as the tuk-tuk swerves down the aisle.

"Tuk-tuk, take me to the place in our mind's eye," Dana cries.

"Sorry," the tuk-tuk says, "I don't recognize your voice."

"Yes, you do!" Dana screams at the speaker, "because you've been hearing my voice for the past several thousand years."

"TUK-TUK!" I scream. We're about three metres from squishing King Henry VIII like a butterfly. "TAKE ME ANYWHERE AWAY FROM HERE!"

Just as we get a close-up view of Henry VIII's nostrils, the portal opens. I scrunch my eyes shut and we soar through, leaving behind the sound of screaming, the organ screeching and someone asking, "Can I take back my air fryer?"

I wait for the familiar bump as we land, but it doesn't come... Weird. Cautiously, I open my eyes. We're floating about in complete darkness, *and* it smells bad, like that time I left a banana peel in my swimming bag all summer.

"I don't want to be a know-it-all," Dana says into the pitch black, "but I don't think that worked."

I blink frantically, but it's no use. I can't see anything.

I can't hear anything either, except for Dana and the beating of our hearts.

"Is this a black hole?" I ask, fright and confusion rising in my voice.

Dana takes a deep breath then says, "You know as well as I do that black holes form when a star dies, not when time-travelling wedding crashers give ambiguous instructions."

I'm too overwhelmed to make sense of Dana's words. What if we're stuck here for the rest of our lives? My heart begins to beat worryingly fast.

"Something has obviously gone very wrong here," Dana remarks.

"Maybe it's the butterfly effect," I ponder. "Perhaps we've caused too many changes in the past and it's making the timeline do weird things."

"But I've been so careful about everything!"

I raise my eyebrows. "Dana, you squished a butterfly, ate apples from Isaac Newton's garden *and* turned Marie Curie into a K-pop fan. It's me who's been careful!"

"You call shaving Shakespeare's iconic beard off being careful? Did you even consider how much his new look went against Queen Elizabeth I's fashion rules?"

"No," I say into the dark, "because fashion shouldn't have rules."

"Look, we need to work together. We both eradicated King Tut from history – we've got to put him back where he belongs."

She's right. This is bigger than us. But how do we escape this not-a-black-hole black hole?

"Maybe the tuk-tuk just didn't know where to go," Dana offers. "You need to have K-Mania clear in your mind's eye. I'll prompt you. So, think fans, think fandom, think mania."

I picture dancing, singing, screaming, exhilaration until it's all I can think about. Then, I say in my most *I mean business* voice, "Tuk-tuk, take me to the place in my mind's eye."

At last, the darkness sinks away and the portal flicks a thousand colours. It's beautiful and dizzying and eye-popping. Dana takes my hand and says, "Keep thinking fandom!"

Soon, the kaleidoscope of colours drains away and the portal flashes black, white and shades of grey. Weird! I turn to Dana: she's in black, white and shades of grey too!

"No way!" I shriek. "You've turned into the olden days."

"You too!" Dana replies.

This doesn't make sense because I was thinking exclusively of fandom and mania and—

POP!

My ears pierce with the deafening sounds of screams as we land in the middle of a crowd of excited fans. We're at a concert.

"AZ8?" I bounce in my seat excitedly, because on reflection we should have spent the weekend time travelling to all the stops on one of AZ8's old world tours.

Dana shakes her head. "This isn't AZ8. I don't think it's K-pop at all."

She's right. There's something off about this concert, and it's not just that everything is still in black-and-white. The fans don't look like Glows at all. They're dressed in smart tops and long skirts and rocking big beehive hairdos. They're all teenage girls, whereas at an AZ8 concert there are people of all ages and genders. Plus, not a single person has a light stick.

"Why does this feel so completely familiar and entirely different at the same time?" Dana yells over the screams.

Yes, exactly that.

We don't dare leave the tuk-tuk so lean out to get a better view of the stage. On it are four men in black suits with matching haircuts. Three of them have guitars and one at the back is on the drums. They're singing – well, at least I *think* they are. It's impossible to hear them over the deafening sound of fans going wild.

"I love this song!" Dana shouts as she wiggles her fingers in the air.

"How can you even hear this song?"

"I can't. I recognize the vibrations!" she yells while bopping her head.

A girl with a super-sweet pixie haircut throws herself against the bonnet of the tuk-tuk and cries, "I love Ringo!"

Another girl, who is in floods of tears, grabs her friend off the boot and aggressively screeches, "Paul is so cute. I want to put him in my pocket."

Ringo? Paul? What kind of boy band names are those?

I look around and— Ah, I get it now. "The Beatles?"

Dana laughs. "Yes! Boy band royalty." She boogies away to the vibrations, and I join in, both of us bopping side to side in our seat until at last, I come to my senses. "We're getting distracted!" I shout.

Dana pauses mid bop, closes her eyes and rubs at her temples.

Think, think, think. But it's impossible to think with all the screaming!

"Tuk-tuk, take us away from here!" I instruct, and

the engine revs instantly. Just as I'm about to panic that we're going to run over a mass of Beatles fans, the portal flashes right in front of us and we dive into the blackness.

"That was *Beatle*mania," Dana reasons, "not *K*-mania."

"If only we could hop on a plane and fly there," I moan, closing my eyes and picturing us in business class on some fancy jet. Suddenly a loud, humming sound causes me to flick open my eyes. Flying directly towards us is an aircraft made entirely from rickety wood and a bunch of bedsheets. "What on earth?"

"It's one of the Wright brothers!" Dana squeals, waving excitedly at a man with an impressive moustache flying the plane. "An aviation pioneer and all-round legend."

It's hard to get excited, though, when it's about to crash into us! Dana screams as I grip the steering wheel and veer us away. Phew! There's no time to get my breath back as something else immediately hurtles into our path and this time, the aircraft is fast, furious and threatening.

"A spitfire!" I shout, as the small fighter aircraft roars closer. My stomach jumps into my throat and Dana and I clutch each other in panic. "We're going to die!" I weep, as it bears down on us, but just as we're about to collide, it tips on its side and thunders past in a flash of green and brown.

"Why is this happening?" Dana asks.

"I was thinking about flights!" I cry, knowing I've gone wrong somewhere.

"Why?" she asks confused.

"I don't know!" I wail, even more confused.

Dana's eyes widen in panic and I turn to see what she's looking at with a sickening dread in my belly. Taking up the whole field of vision is a jumbo jet...

There's no dodging this. We scream as its nose comes terrifyingly close, its pilot stopping with a half-eaten doughnut in her hand to stare at us in complete bewilderment. "Tuk-tuk!" I shout. "Take me to K-mania. Now!"

We jump again, then again, then again. For a split second we're at a party, a parade, a bustling marketplace, a nightclub we are most certainly too young to be in. At one point we're even on the runway of a fashion show, cameras flashing and fancy people applauding. Jump, jump, jump, not stopping to take anything in, like when you hold your finger on the up button on the remote and go through all the channels as fast as you can. My head spins, I close my eyes and yell, "K-Mania! K-Mania! K-Mania!"

And then...

POP!

16
K-MANIA ... AGAIN

"Did we die?"

I open my eyes and look around at the beautiful sight of fandom. "We're alive," I sing joyfully.

"Are you sure?" Dana asks as she raises her head from between her legs.

"Definitely alive! Look!" I hop out of the tuk-tuk and throw my hands in the air. "We're back at K-Mania! We did it, Dana! We did it."

Dana staggers out of the tuk-tuk and drops to her knees. "Thank you," she mumbles as she kisses the pavement in front of the convention centre.

I laugh. "I thought you were against getting up close and personal with pavement germs."

She stands and straightens out her long black lab coat. "I was. But after being lost in time for the last five centuries, I'm extremely happy to be home."

Above the entrance of the conference centre a digital screen flashes:

DAY TWO K-MANIA

I grab my photobook from the back seat and tuck it tightly under an arm. K-pop fans are great people, but they also tend to be on the fanatical side and this book is worth a lot of money. There's no way I'm letting it out of my sight today.

"So, here's the plan," Dana says, as she switches into full Dana mode. "We find Tut, then go back in time to drop him off, then forward in time to find your nana and then forward-forward to get back here to see Lilac Eyes do a rousing performance of 'Water' and get your limited-edition AZ8 wooden chopping board."

I nod doubtfully, because while this *does* sound like a watertight plan, as the hours tick by, I'm less and less confident about the finding Nana part.

"What's wrong?" Dana asks. "Why do you look so unsure?"

I take a deep, shaky breath.

"Skylar?" Dana narrows her eyes at me. "What's going on?"

"I don't remember where we left Nana," I blurt. "I

can't see it. The place. It was too generic. It was just some wide-open green space with grass and a house and—"

"A disgusting fluttery minibeast."

I stare down at my feet and the horrible truth falls out. "I'm worried it's not specific enough, that when I ask the tuk-tuk to take me to the place in my mind's eye, it won't be able to find it. Getting to K-Mania was difficult enough."

Dana puts a hand on my shoulder. "Don't worry – we'll work it out together; we always work things out together. We'll find her even if it means we must spend the rest of the afternoon, or indeed the rest of our lives, searching."

I look up at my bestie's smiling, encouraging face. "You'd do that for me?"

"That's what besties are—"

"Hey!" a long-haired boy dressed as a Bad Cake yells at us. "I want seven banging breakfast burritos right now. One with extra cheese, hold the beans. Another with vegan sausage, vegan chicken, vegan egg and extra bacon, another with—"

"No," Dana says simply.

"Excuse me, what did you say?" the boy asks, in a rather menacing tone. Behind him other Bad Cakes emerge, all of them equally peckish *and* unfriendly.

Dana stands her ground. "We're sold out."

"Sold out?" a sassy girl from the group says. She puts her hands on her hips and tuts her teeth. "This is unacceptable."

I step towards the complaining girl. "Do you have any idea how much history hangs on us staying focused right now?"

"I'm going to leave you a terrible review online." The girl snaps a photo of the tuk-tuk. "*Purrito's Burritos*, huh? You should watch out."

Dana grabs my hand, and we make our way up the stairs and towards the entrance to get our tickets scanned.

"Goodness Greta!" Dana cries as she jabs a finger towards a bright light.

"Greta Thunberg's a K-pop fan?" I ask, surprised at this little-known fact.

"No, it's Darcy from K-popdontstop.com!"

Indeed, standing a few metres away is the legend herself, in all her pink-haired and high fashion glory. Today she's wearing green contact lenses, sticky forehead gems and long feathery blue eyelashes. She's so naturally stunning.

"Hey peeps," she delivers to her assistant holding

a top-of-the-range phone and halo light. "It's your girl, Darcy Delaney from K-popdontstop.com, your one-stop shop for all K-pop news, reviews and possible untruths. I'm back here for Day Two of K-Mania. Later on, I'll be interviewing the rich, famous and fabulous, but right now, let's chat to some poor, non-famous normal people." Darcy shifts her heavy feathery eyes around the crowd before landing in our direction. "Coo-ee!" she calls. "Normal people? Hello?"

"Us?" I say, gesturing to myself and Dana. Surely not. Because while we're unmistakably normal, we've also not had a bath all weekend.

Darcy shuffles closer and grins her perfectly white teeth. "Come and say hi to my millions of viewers."

Half blinded by the halo light, I wave awkwardly at the camera.

"What an unusual look you're rocking here," Darcy says, as she eyes Dana's dusty black lab coat. "I can't even guess what fandom you're part of. Who are you here to see today?"

Despite being asked a direct question, Dana doesn't reply. Unless you count a tight, boxy smile as a reply. This is exactly like the time she got interviewed by local news after she guerilla planted wildflowers at every bus stop.

I nudge her. "You need to open your mouth to speak."

Dana proves she's listening by opening her mouth, yet no sound comes out.

"We're Glows," I tell Darcy's viewers.

Darcy pretends to cry. "Ah, sucks to be you. I'm sorry."

"Don't be," I snap. "I'm a Glow for life."

"Right, right," Darcy nods. "Even though AZ8 are *taking a break*" – she bunny ears the words – "which we all know is boy band language for *we hate each other and don't want to hang out and make cheesy songs for girls anymore*. Ha ha ha."

I gasp. I redden. I near explode. "Let me stop you right there, Darcy, because … because…" And then, I don't know what comes over me, perhaps it's because I skipped a full breakfast, or didn't sleep very well in the seventeenth century, or maybe I'm not as reassured by Dana's words as I thought I was, but I start to weep.

Dana puts an arm around me. "Don't cry," she whispers.

"I can't help it. Say if she's right – say if AZ8 never get back together, and everyone moves on and leaves the fandom and then it's just me, by myself?"

"That's not going to happen, Skylar. AZ8 said they're taking a break – you've got to trust them. But if they change their minds and don't get back together then that's OK too. Because you'll still have the music and the memories. You'll also have the possibility of eight solo albums."

There's laughter from beside us. I almost forgot Darcy was still here. "Great pep talk, kid," she says spitefully, "but pop moves fast. You really think anyone wants to listen to yesterday's music? No way, especially boy bands: they're as disposable as a plastic bag."

Now, Dana is the one near explosion. "There is nothing, I repeat NOTHING, disposable about something that takes two decades to fully decompose. What do you people not understand about microplastics ruining the seas?" Dana grabs the camera and shouts into it, "Does no one care about the effect of plastic on Prochlorococcus?"

Yikes! When Dana starts shouting off about bacteria, I know it's time to move on. I take the camera and hand it back to a shocked Darcy.

"Tote bags for life!" Dana yells as I drag her kicking and screaming into the main hall.

Once we're far away from mean Darcy and the brightness of the halo light, we both begin to calm down. "Are you OK?" Dana asks me in a gentle voice.

"Are *you* OK?" I ask. "Because I don't know who's more likely to go viral from that."

We both laugh then gaze around the arena. There

are more people here than yesterday and the atmosphere feels super electric.

"Thanks for what you said back there," I say to Dana.

"It was nothing. She was hugely misinformed. I mean, we literally went to a boy band concert from over sixty years ago and heard a song that still gets played today. AZ8 will be for life too." She flips a finger heart at me, and my actual heart feels all fuzzy. "Now, the most important thing we need to do is stay focused," she adds.

I nod in agreement. Yes: focus. No more crying or ranting on live feeds. We need to find Tut. I stop the nearest passing stranger. "Excuse me, have you seen a small ancient Egyptian boy round here?"

"What does he look like?"

"Umm." I get out my phone, and my shoulders drop. "It's completely flat."

"Mine too," Dana says.

"Tough going," the stranger says. "There are charging lockers over there."

We run over to the lockers and I rest my photobook on the top as I try to help Dana with a dodgy cable. Once the phones are safely charging, we make our way to the K-Mania Marketplace. "Doh! I left my photobook on top of the charging locker." I race back, relieved to find it exactly where I left it.

As we wander through the marketplace, Dana takes a deep breath and declares, "I feel so much fresher without being distracted by my phone. I swear I can feel the fractures in my attention span healing." She rubs her temples and grins.

"Me too," I say, rubbing my own head, because she's right: I feel super fresh.

"Cool, so let's split up. Meet back here in an hour?"

I fire her a thumbs up. "Great plan."

We go our separate ways, phoneless and focused.

"Nothing can distract me," I mumble as I pass a stall making fresh doughnuts. They smell amazing but no, focus is my middle name.

"Excuse me, excuse me," I ask every person I pass. "Can you assist, urgent situation here, a minor has been lost. Have you seen him?"

Then I spot a small desk set up in front of the toilets. Lost and Found. Yes! I can't believe I didn't think of this earlier – it's so obvious.

"Hello," I say to the lady at the desk, who is busy sorting piles of umbrellas. "Can you help me? I've lost something."

"Was it an umbrella?" she asks. "Because here." She hands me a random brolly.

"Oh, no, it's actually a person, a small ruler from an

ancient civilization to be more specific."

The lady pushes her glasses up her nose. "Can you describe this small ruler?"

I rest my photobook on her desk to give my arms a break. "Small, swaggy and possibly carrying a slightly overweight ginger cat. Some would say he looks like Tutankhamun – you know the famous ancient Egyptian boy king?" I wait for her reaction.

She puts a tag on an umbrella and chucks it in a cupboard. "Never heard of him."

I recoil with a huge gasp. Even though we'd already established this disaster, a little part of me had thought Dana was being overdramatic. But no, the butterfly effect is real!

"Are you sure?" I ask the lady. "Because Tutankhamun is one of the most famous figures in history."

"Listen kid, I have a degree in History, and I've never heard of any KooKa Ka Moon."

I lean heavily on the desk as I feel the weight of this. "Never mind. Thank you for your help."

As I walk off, trying to figure out my next move, the lady calls me back. "Hey, kid!" she shouts. "You left your photobook: hold onto it or it'll end up in my cupboard of brollies."

How do I keep forgetting something so precious?

I think of Nana, lost in time and possibly furious with me. Then I think of Tut's family and friends back in ancient Egypt; they must be so worried about him. With a burst of energy, I realize it's up to me to put things right.

I march on through the marketplace, past hundreds of stalls of both handmade and official merchandise. "I'm going to put things right, I'm going to—"

A tall boy with a green buzzcut steps out in front of me. "Do you want to join my K-pop bracelet making workshop?"

"I one hundred per cent do," I answer, "but I'm doing something very, very important right now."

"More important than checking out our new eco-friendly UV glow-in-the-dark beads?" The boy raises his wrists to display an astonishing stripey rainbow of beaded bracelets.

"Ooh," I coo, "nice collection. And did you say eco-friendly? My bestie would love this." I rest myself down on a stool, just for a moment. "It's like a sweet shop," I say, gazing at the thousands of beads.

"Yes, but instead of being deliciously edible, everything is fashionably sustainable." The boy hands me a string and I try to decide what colour beads to go for.

"Wow, what a stunning photobook, do you mind

if I take a peek?" He reaches out for it, and I tighten my grip.

"Slow down there, Kermit. I'll supervise you once I complete these crafts."

I tuck my photobook between my feet as I make Dana a bracelet from reclaimed wood with the words I HEART EARTH, and myself a glow-in-the-dark one which spells out GLOW4EVA.

This is so relaxing. I could literally sit here all day.

Dana runs over, breaking the calm. "Skylar, what are you doing?"

"Crafting," I answer, as I lift my creations. "Wanna join? Or do you fancy getting some bibimbap? The smell of fried egg from that Korean food stall over there has been taunting me ever since I sat down."

"Nooooo!" Dana screams, shattering the serenity of the bracelet making stall. "It can't be!" She pushes her fingers into her hair as she stares beyond me. I turn my head to see the source of her dramatics and … oh. A digital screen is flashing with a K-Mania announcement:

Eight per cent discount on rucksacks shaped as feline heads. One-time offer. Today only.

"You want to cash in on that?" I ask Dana, a little confused by her extreme reaction.

"No!" She points again at the screen, and I swivel round to look.

Today's Lilac Eyes performance has been cancelled. We apologize for any inconvenience.

"Why?" Dana sobs. "Why, why, why?"

"Oh, is that the girl group?" Green Hair asks as he warms up his glue gun. "I heard their flight got caught up in all that crazy stuff with air traffic control earlier. A small flying green object almost crashed into a jumbo jet. I'm calling it now: that was some alien business."

As I consider how the tuk-tuk could easily be described as a "small flying green object", Dana sinks down onto the stool opposite me and her shoulders hunch in despair.

"I'm so sorry," I say.

"It's fine," she replies sadly. "I'm sure there will be plenty more chances to see them. Even though K-pop bands only come to Britain every four years and when they do the tickets are a bajillion pounds."

I pull a tray of beads onto my lap and decide to craft Dana something special to cheer her up. As I'm very carefully tying the string, she screams again, causing me to flinch. "What now?" I ask.

This time, her eyes are filled with shock as she stares at the digital screen and points.

The display flashes with an illustration of someone putting a plushie down the toilet and a big red cross over it. The message reads:

Upstairs toilets closed until further notice.

I turn back to her. "Dana, I really don't see how that's relevant right now."

She takes my head in her hot hands and swivels it back just in time to see a giant image of Tut on the screen. He's giving an intense look, his eyeliner is thicker than usual and he's definitely been airbrushed. Though more distracting is the fact he's holding Kookie in his arms and the tagline reads:

Introducing Tut. An idol for a new generation, debuting today at 2 p.m. on the Future Stage. Only at K-Mania.

17
LETTING GO

"What on earth?" I gulp. "I can't believe this!"

"I know," Dana says angrily as she ties on my bracelet. "How dare he replace Lilac Eyes as the headlining act on the Future Stage."

"No, I meant how has he managed to build himself as a K-idol in less than twenty-four hours despite not being Korean and not *even* being alive? And more importantly, how could he approve that horrible photo of Kookie?"

On the screen, my beautiful Kookie has been caught unawares with her tiny pink tongue poking out.

"Wait up a time-travelling minute," Dana says as she looks around. "What are we doing? Why are we sitting here putting on accessories? We're meant to be saving history."

I glance down at the tray of beads on my lap, and while the bead selection *is* fabulous, she's right.

We both jump up at the same time, which is extra dramatic as the beads on my lap go flying in the air before raining down all over the floor. Whoops.

"I'm so sorry," I tell Green Hair as millions of tiny beads scatter everywhere. I try, in vain, to scoop up as many as possible but I literally do not have the time. "So sorry," I say again as he shakes his glue gun at me, "I need to go."

Dana pulls me up and we try to make our getaway, slipping and sliding precariously on the beads. After nearly faceplanting multiple times, we manage to steady ourselves and make it to the edge of the bead pit. Then we run and run, dashing through crowds across K-Mania in search of the Future Stage.

"I don't think I can run anymore!" Dana cries from behind me, and I spin to see her bent over and huffing. "I'm out of energy. I need food. Water. A passionfruit mochi ice cream."

"You can have all those things *after*," I tell her. "*After* we save history."

Dana forces herself forward and we run to the Future Stage, pushing through to the front of the crowd, which is rude but completely necessary when the situation is as desperate as this. Once we're as close as possible, I survey the crowd. Everyone is standing shoulder to shoulder with their phones poised in hands, ready to film. I can't believe Tut has pulled so many people.

"They don't even know who he is," I say to Dana. "Why are they all so excited to see him?"

A tall guy in a tiger T-shirt nudges me. "Tut went viral last night for an impromptu dance routine outside of Buckingham Palace."

"HE WHAT?" Dana and I holler.

"Yeah, he did a triple backflip while wearing a crown. And the crown didn't fall off."

A blue-haired girl in a Bad Cakes hoodie adds, "I've heard Tut's vocal range is eight octaves and he can sing higher than dolphins. He's already a legend if you ask me."

"Yeah, K-pop has gone up a notch as far as skills. Much better than seeing another girl group," the boy guffaws.

Dana's face goes a little red.

"Ignore them," I tell her.

She glares at the empty stage. "I know we said we want to give Tut a moment to be a normal kid, but this has gone too far."

"I agree. He needs to get his ancient butt back on the throne. His own throne. In the past. Where he belongs. Where he—"

"Yes, I get it. I get it," Dana interrupts, her arms crossed angrily. "Lilac Eyes have been training for this moment for ever, and then some random boy king swoops in and scoops it up."

Suddenly the stage fades to a sandy yellow. Oh! *Real* sand is pouring down from filters in the ceiling. Then, on a big screen at the back of the stage, an image appears of something running. It gets bigger and bigger as it gets closer to the screen, until it's recognisable as a chubby ginger cat. *My* chubby ginger cat!

"Kookie?!" I say in disbelief.

She gallops like a leopard, though with far less grace and poise.

Over the speakers a booming voice proclaims, "From a distant land comes an icon to last generations. A talent like no other. Behold, the future of music."

"Exaggerate much?" I scoff.

"Yeah," Dana agrees, still refusing to unfold her arms, despite people bashing her as they surge forward.

An army of dancers march on, all of them in gold flowing robes. I don't know how they're going to dance in those; I once tried to do the shuffle in an ankle-length skirt and got into all kinds of trouble.

The dancers form a long line across the stage, then part in the middle as a shadowy figure emerges from a trapdoor. Their face is covered in a shimmering gold scarf. As a wind machine starts, the scarf blows away to reveal—

"Tut!" the audience screams in delight.

Tut doesn't move, just stands there basking in the audience's completely over-the-top response to him doing … well, nothing.

Eventually, he drops to his knees as if in prayer and sings a capella, "*You break me, you take me.*"

"How'd he learn English so fast?" I ask Dana.

Slowly, dramatically, he peels himself from the ground and croons, "*You bake me a sand witch.*"

"Oh," I say, "I take it back, he hasn't learned English."

Then, the beat drops, the guitars go ballistic, the drummer loses all control and Tut lifts his gold cane in the air and hollers, "Sand time. Let's go!"

The audience go wild, and I have no choice but to put my fingers in my ears like my dad does when I sing.

"*Some mayo, with love, some pickle and cabbage. Habibi, Habibi, woooo-set me free-ee.*" Tut runs across the stage, getting a huge cheer from those on the left, then those on the right.

"Who does he think he is?" I shout. "This is way over the top."

Tut sashays to the front of the stage where he

reaches down to touch the raised hand of one fangirl, who promptly faints. His eyes snag on me getting squashed up by the barricade and he breaks character for a moment to send us a double thumbs up.

"He saw us!" Dana says, her tone switching from annoyed to flattered.

"Who cares?" I say through gritted teeth, "we don't have time for this."

"He's pretty good." Dana sways along with Tut's silky-smooth vocals. "Not as good as Lilac Eyes, but still… *Habibi Habibi*," she sings.

"Stop habibi-ing."

Tut reaches under his cape and grabs at something. He looks down into the crowd with a questioning smile. In response the crowd chant, "Do it! Do it!"

"Do what?" I ask Dana.

"Do it! Do it!"

Tut chucks a large handful of bright yellow sand in the air. It looks spectacular and everyone tries to get a photo of it. Then the sand falls and, "Err, pfft," I spit.

"He's wonderful!" blue-haired girl squeals hysterically while wiping sand from her watering eyes.

Tut moonwalks across the stage, stops to bounce his shoulders, then moonwalks back the other way. "You want sand witches?" he shouts. Again, another handful of sand. Everyone loves it, despite having to close their eyes.

He then does something I've only ever seen on television. He turns around and falls backwards into the waiting hands of thousands of fans. Still mic'd up, he continues to croon, *"Habibi, Habibi, carry me like the sea-ee."*

"Crowd surfing is not very K-pop!" I shout. "Can you imagine Haru doing this?"

"No," Dana says, with her eyes glued on Tut. "Because if Haru did this, someone would literally steal him."

"Yeah, me!" I laugh. "I'd put him in my pocket because he's the cutest little K-pop idol in the world and— Whoa, no, stop!" My precious photobook has been taken out of my hands and is now in the air, being passed from one set of grabby hands to another. It's basically crowd surfing.

My neck creaks with the strain of having to keep up with the location of Tut and my photobook. "Stop!" I yell. "It's mine, give it back." I try to jump and reach it but it's no use. Being short really has its downsides. Then, a wriggly mass of gold makes its way over: Tut.

When he's right above us we tug him down to standing and his eyes light up. "Slave!" he delights, then grabs Dana for an unexpected hug. I notice how her face goes extra red. Tut pulls away, looks at me and says, "And you, number two!" I also get hugged, and it softens me a bit.

"Home time?" he asks hopefully.

Poor Tut. I feel bad for leaving him here this long.

Someone knocks my side and when I look, it's blue-haired girl. "Here," she says, handing me my photobook.

"Thank you," I cry as I stroke its cover which is now a little moist from everyone's clammy hands. "Thank you, thank—"

"It's cool," she says dismissively. "No one likes AZ8 anymore."

Before I can launch into my "oh, yes they do" lecture, Dana takes my hand. She's already dragging Tut with her other hand, and together the three of us push through the crowds, which is not easy with Tut in tow.

"Woo, we love you!"

"Can I have your autograph?"

"Please stop for a selfie."

"Urgh," I moan, "these fans are so over the top." I drop my head to avoid being filmed. It's an uncomfortable feeling. I really don't like being the focus of a sea of phones. This must be how AZ8 feel all the time – no wonder they're taking a break.

As we near the exit I spot a problem. "How are we going to do the whole disappearing tuk-tuk thing with this many eyes on us?"

Dana too now looks around at the crowd trailing us. "We can't. We need to lose them somehow."

Out of nowhere Kookie comes bounding over and jumps into Tut's arms. "Habibi!" Tut cries, delighted.

The crowd closes in and we make a break for it through a fire exit, slamming the door shut behind us. While running down a long grey corridor, I remember something: "Our phones are still in the charging lockers."

"We'll get them later," Dana huffs.

"Later, yes," Tut puffs. "Then slave make sand witch."

We burst through another door, which luckily takes us outside the convention centre, but as we race closer to the spot we parked in, another problem rears its ugly head.

The tuk-tuk: it's gone!

In its place stands the group of Bad Cakes from earlier.

"Where's our vehicle?" I demand.

They laugh. "You might want to check over there," a tattooed boy sneers as he points to the main road where a big tow truck is making off with our tuk-tuk!

"Arghhh!"

So, despite our depleting energy, thirst, hunger and general state of complete overstimulation, the three of us run like our lives depend on it. Because in a way, they kind of do.

Tut is the slowest, not only because he uses a cane, but because he's carrying a feline the same weight as a bowling ball.

"Tired," he pants, while cuddling Kookie to his chest. "Need. Slave. To. Carry."

"Idols don't get tired." I grab Kookie and place her under my free arm.

"*Neeowww!*" Kookie wails.

The tow truck seems impossibly far away. Then, as if the K-pop gods are on our side, a traffic light ahead turns red, forcing the tow truck to stop. Dana strides forward and reaches the tuk-tuk, jumping in over the boot and sliding into the back seat like some kind of *Fast & Furious* stunt double. I'm impressed.

Somehow Tut bounds ahead of me. Dana stretches her arms out for him to get in next. He chucks in his stick, then with his striking dancer's agility does a flying flip into the back seat, laughing as he tumbles in.

"Skylar, quick!" Dana shouts. "The lights are about to turn green."

I'm almost there, but my beloved photobook and

darling cat are weighing me down. As I run and run, my beaded bracelets clack, my eyebrows sweat and my perspiring feet squeak in two-day-old socks.

"Faster!" Dana shouts.

"Come," Tut says. "Home time."

Home? I can't think of a more glorious idea. Except maybe sharing a fried chicken buffet with AZ8.

"FASTER!"

"HOME!"

The lights change and the tow truck starts to move off.

"Nooooooo!" I yell. From deep inside I pull up my last kilowatt of energy to close the distance. Tut's hands are outstretched as he beckons either me or, more likely, Kookie, to catch up.

"Drop the weight!" Dana yells, as she and Tut begin to shrink from view.

I glance at the loads in my arms. Has it really come to this? My photobook or Kookie? It's the more serious version of someone saying pizza: pineapple or anchovies? How is anyone meant to choose?

Dana leans right out of the tuk-tuk as Tut holds onto her legs. Whoa, she really should consider becoming a stunt double if the whole Nobel Prize and saving the world thing doesn't work out.

"Run!" she screams. "Skylar, run!"

"I am!" I cry.

"*Neeowww*!" Kookie yowls.

I then put all my PE skills into action as I perform an epic overarm throw, just like I did with baby Tae yesterday. Kookie goes flying through the air, before landing in the tuk-tuk, knocking Tut backwards.

"Drop the photobook!" Dana yells, as her fingers strain towards me.

"I can't. This is hundreds of pounds worth of high-quality, high-gloss-printed card."

"It's time!" Dana shrieks, as the tuk-tuk gets tossed left and right. "Skylar, please. Stop holding onto things."

I feel the photobook slip from my grasp as my hands get sweaty. I can't do it. I can't discard AZ8 like they mean nothing to me.

"Skylar, you have to let go."

I drop the photobook, then jump forward and grab Dana by her hands.

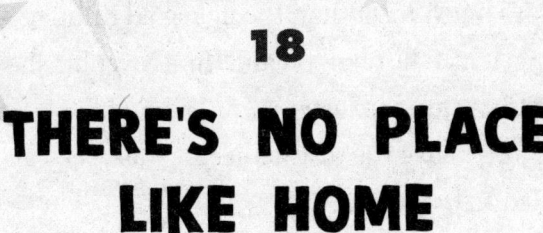

18

THERE'S NO PLACE LIKE HOME

With all of us filling our minds' eye with ancient Egypt, blasting back to 1331BC is a breeze. We land in the sand – obviously – a short walk away from the sphinx-guarded arch.

As we step out of the tuk-tuk, Tut picks up Kookie for one last nuzzle. It's kind of sweet, even if it does last, in my opinion, an inappropriately long time.

"Aww," Dana says, "they've bonded."

Eventually, he gives Kookie a kiss on her furry head, then places her back in the tuk-tuk.

"Hope you enjoyed your *fun time*," I say to him.

He grins widely, then does a perfect pirouette. In the sand! He is so boy band material. I applaud and he takes a bow. Then, another one. And another one.

"OK, Tut, stop milking it." I step forward to tie my glow-in-the-dark GLOW4EVA bracelet around his wrist. It's much nicer than the ugly gold thing he's been wearing, which he takes off and flings over his shoulder.

He then turns to Dana. "You," he says.

Uh-oh! I have the distinct feeling *someone's* about to be called a slave again.

Tut brings his fist in front of his mouth and blows on it three times, before producing a finger heart. "For friend."

Dana chokes up. "Thank you," she says, returning the blow-up heart. "You're my friend too. Bye, Tut."

Dana and I put our arms around each other as we watch Tut skip off, back to his family, kingdom and eventual death.

"He's the sweetest boy in the world," Dana says. "I'm really going to miss him."

"Me too."

Well, that was surprisingly easy. Though somehow, I don't think finding Nana will be quite so simple… I take a deep breath, Dana takes a deep breath and even Kookie takes a deep breath.

"Here we go," I say, my voice wobbling as we all get back in the tuk-tuk. "What if we can't find her? What if she's lost for ever?" My heart beats fast.

Dana pats my knee. "We can do this."

"I know that's your lying voice."

"I'm not lying; I believe it. Look at what we've already achieved this weekend. We helped Tut have fun. We cured Curie's mind block. We even saved a woman from being executed. And now we're going to find your nana. Sure, we might not get home in time for dinner tonight, or ever, but—"

Suddenly, a glitter bomb goes off in my head. "Wowsers!" I scream.

"What?" Dana screams back.

"That's it. That's where Nana's gone." My hands shake as the realisation hits me. "She's gone home."

Dana frowns. "No, she couldn't have gone home. Not without the tuk-tuk."

"Not home *home*," I explain. "She's gone to her home *home* home. Her childhood home."

"You're a genius!" Dana hoots as she gives me a high five.

"Why didn't we think of this before?" I say, bouncing in my seat. "She's always telling stories about it, *and* she said something about getting a recipe." I buckle up and hit the red button.

This should be easy now: I don't have to picture some generic grassy space; all I have to do is picture details from any of the confusing, wandering stories Nana has ever told me about her childhood. I close my eyes and say, "Tuk-tuk, take us to the place in my mind's eye. Take us to Nana's home *home* home."

As we land in the wide-open green space, my nerves kick in. I don't think I'm ready to deal with the repercussions of going off time travelling unsupervised all weekend. I can't even imagine the punishment for such a thing. Will it be a K-pop ban? Total screen ban? Family time ban where I'm banished to my box room while everyone plays board games without me?

A gentle hand on my arm snaps me out of these spiralling thoughts. "You can do it, Skylar," Dana says encouragingly.

I nod. "Yes. Right. Of course. I can do it." I step out of the tuk-tuk, then pause. "What about you – are you going to be all right out here with all the butterflies?"

Dana jumps down onto a patch of scrubby grass and gets into lotus pose. "Yes, because I'm going to meditate." Her eyes flutter closed. "Ommm!"

I was kind of hoping she would come with me. Never mind. I walk towards the pale pink house alone. I stop in front of one of the windows, which is covered with pink wooden slats. Just as I'm about to peek through, a large one-eared rabbit bounces into my path. "Akua?" I ask, though of course I get no response because Akua *is* a rabbit.

I tiptoe into the house and am immediately hit with the smell of fried onions and spices.

"Hello?" I call. "Anyone home?"

I carry on through to a living room filled with big wooden benches which are piled with colourfully patterned cushions. On a side table, a fancy blue trilby hat sits.

Hmm. Where is everyone?

"Goo goo!" a small voice says.

I look down and there's the cutest little sheesh-moo I've ever seen in my life.

"Hello there," I coo.

The baby's wearing a bright orange babygrow and matching orange bonnet. Too cute. In response to the "eee" sound I let out, she gurgles and blinks her big baby eyes at me.

"Aren't you a little cutie patootie," I say as I kneel next to her on the raffia floor mat. "What's your name?"

"Her name is Nana," a serious voice says.

I jump back up. Standing there, in the doorway, arms folded and looking incredibly cross, is … Nana.

"Whoa!" I say. "That was such a dramatic entrance."

I'm shocked, terrified and a little confused. Where to start? "Nana, I'm sorry, I'm—"

I falter under her angry stare. This is worse than I thought. Then after a few seconds, her face cracks into a smile and, as much as I know I have a lot of explaining to do, right now what I want more than anything is one of her garlicky-smelling hugs. Her arms open and I run into them.

"Skylar, do you realize you've been gone for over twenty-four hours?" she says into my hair.

"Really?" I say, my voice wobbling. "It felt longer."

"I was starting to think you'd never come back for me."

"Of course I came back for you. It just took me a while to work out where you were."

She pulls away to look at me, then down at the baby, and her eyes light up.

Something dawns on me. "Ohmygoodness!" I squeal. "Are you that baby? I mean, is that baby you?"

Nana chuckles.

"Did you time travel in order to see *yourself* as a baby?"

Baby Nana joins in with the chuckling.

"I time travelled here to get the recipe for the spinach stew my mum used to make. And, I guess yes, I wanted to see my childhood home again." Nana sits on one of the sofas and gestures for me to join her.

"Why didn't you tell me you wanted to come here?" I ask. "Why keep it a secret?"

"I was a bit worried," she says. "I didn't want you to think I don't love my home with you in London. I love my life and family there. But I also miss my *home*. Do you understand?"

"I get it," I say, because you know what, I'm mighty mature.

"Booboo," baby Nana says.

"Ohmygosh," I say. "You were sooo cute."

"I know, right," Nana says.

Just then, another person appears in the doorway. She's wearing an old-fashioned pink housedress with a matching pink headwrap and looks weirdly like Nana. And by this, I mean present-day Nana, not baby Nana, if you're following.

"Skylar, this is Mrs Smith. The baby's mother. Mrs Smith, this is…" Nana stalls as she gestures towards me. "A mysterious stranger."

Mrs Smith smiles. "Are you hungry, mysterious stranger?"

"I think so," I nod, wishing Dana was here because I need extra brainpower to process all this. So, this lady, Mrs Smith, must be Nana's mum, because Nana is also Mrs Smith, which makes the original Mrs Smith my great-grandmother. Whoa!

Great-grandmother Smith leaves, then returns with two plates of steaming spinach stew and bright white yams. All I've had today are a couple of periwinkles, and I'm suddenly ravenous. I take a mouthful and, "Oh whoa, this is…" I take another swallow as I search for the words to describe this most deliciousness. "Mmm, like eating gold."

"See," Nana says enthusiastically, "isn't it the most delicious thing you've ever had in your life?"

"Hundred per cent yes," I answer. "What's in this? I can taste habanero pepper, garlic, ginger…"

Nana nods along as baby Nana crawls over to beg for a bite.

I can't stop eating. "Is there even a smidgen of peanut butter?"

"Yes, yes," Nana approves. "Skylar, I'm impressed with your palate."

"Well, I do spend most of my leisure time in the kitchen being your assistant," I moan. "Or at least, I used to."

Nana stops, spoon halfway to her mouth. "You miss it, don't you? You miss cooking with me?"

"I don't miss the cooking part, but maybe I miss the *with you* part."

"Thank you again," Nana says to Mrs Smith as she hugs her at the door.

Baby Nana waves a chubby hand and says, "Booboo."

"By the way," I say as we walk towards the tuk-tuk, "who did Mrs Smith think *you* were?"

"A mysterious stranger," Nana says as she clutches an extra plate of leftovers.

When we get to the tuk-tuk, Dana is still sitting in lotus pose and there's a giant orange butterfly on her nose.

"Up you get," Nana says. "I brought you some food."

"Dana can't get up right now," Dana says in a zoned-out voice. "Dana has ascended to another plane of existence. Dana also has cramp."

Nana waves the plate of food under Dana's nose, and she jumps up. "For me? It smells moreish."

We all get in the tuk-tuk. Kookie curls on my lap, Dana tucks into her food and Nana hits the red button. I smile. I may not have my photobook, but at least I have my best friend and my nana back.

"So," Nana starts as she looks at me in her rearview

mirror, "did you have an excellent adventure in *my* time machine?"

"Errr…" I reply.

Nana laughs. She revs the engine then says, "I once had an adventure. I was twelve. Or maybe eleven. There was a tuna shortage that summer. I'd just cut my hair and…"

Nana's story lasts all the way home *home*.

19

TINGA TINGA TINGA

We touch down outside my house and everyone gives out a relieved sigh. We're back! It feels wonderful to step out of the tuk-tuk and I vow never to accept a lift in it ever again. Then, I remember something. "Our phones!"

Dana clutches at her chest. "My baby! How did I ever forget about it?"

"We left them in the charging lockers at K-Mania."

"I can drive you there," Nana says.

"In that thing?" I laugh, surprised she'd suggest it after all the trouble it's caused. "I don't think so. I'd rather get the bus."

"I'd rather get in a gas-guzzling SUV," Dana says.

"I'd rather jog," I retort. "With Dad. While he reels off facts about past Olympic games."

Nana tuts at us. "Gah! Don't be so silly, girls. I'll

drive very safely and slowly and within this era." She sticks both of her pinkies out. "Dinky deal?"

We don't have that many options, I guess. We each take one of her pinkies and jump back in.

Maybe it's the lingering smell of steak and cheese burritos or the sensation of the wind gently lapping at her fur, but Kookie seems to enjoy the ride. I do too – it's a chance to forget everything terrible that's happened over the last three days slash 3,000 years. The falling out with Dana, the possibility of being exposed to radioactive materials and, worst of all, the loss of my photobook.

When we arrive back at K-Mania, the staff are taking down the banners, emptying the bins and sweeping up. We walk through to the main hall, where all the stalls are packing up and Dana tells me to wait as she runs over to the charging lockers.

"My, my, my," I say disapprovingly, "there are a lot of beads on the floor."

"Hey, kid," a voice calls. I look over to see the lady from the lost property desk. "Did you find your lost ruler?" She laughs as she puts on her jacket.

"Yes, thank you. Turns out he was burning it up on the Future Stage."

"Been there, done that," she says as she pushes her

glasses up. "Glad you found him. Have a good evening."

"Before you go," I call. "I don't suppose anyone handed in an AZ8 photobook, did they?"

The lady shakes her head. "No, but I do have an AZ8 umbrella if you're interested?"

"No thanks, I already have eight of those myself."

She shrugs, then carefully steps her way over the mess of beads, sand and general debris towards the exit.

Dana comes back and hands me my phone. I switch it on, though it's not like there's anything of any interest on the Internet these days.

"Hello, old friend," Dana says as her phone chimes to life. "Oh, how I've missed beaming a constant stream of information directly into my brain."

"What happened to healing your fractured attention span?" I ask.

Dana snorts. "I have so much to catch up on. You have no idea how fast the youth eco movement moves."

With Dana glued to her screen, I check AZ8's social account. Just as I thought. Nothing. No vlogs, no lives, no music and no photos of them looking extraordinary. I guess they really are having a break.

Then, ping, ping, ping. Messages from the next set of important people in the world: my family.

Mum: Hey Skylar. On my way back. Missed you lots. Hope you've been good for Nana. Pizza for dinner?

Dad: Be home by 7. Exhausted. I'll be needing a foot massage from my favourite daughter.

Gross.

I even have a message from my big brother.

Jesse: Can you explain why my bed is full of sand?!

As I'm reading, I mistakenly bump straight into someone. "Sorry," I mumble.

"Excuse me," the person says in an accent I recognize as Korean. "Do you know where lost property is?"

I look up. It's an older girl I recognize but can't think where from. She has long black hair plaited into pigtails, glittery cheeks and she's wearing a very cute T-shirt with a tabby cat on the front. Behind her stand three other older girls, all with equally cute hairstyles, face emblems and cute animal T-shirts.

"What did you say?" I ask, because A: I wasn't concentrating and B: I'm so distracted by how cool they all are.

"I asked if you know where lost property is?"

"I do, but it's closed for the day."

"Oh shoot," she says, with a little stamp of her foot.

"Sorry. K-Mania is over."

"Oh, I know that," the girl says. "We were meant to perform but our flight got held up. Apparently, there was an unidentified flying green object causing havoc in the skies. Very weird."

Perform? Held up? Unidentified flying green object?

Something clicks in my mind, but not quite. I turn to Dana to see if she too is picking up on something peculiar, but she's still getting reacquainted with her phone. I nudge her and she shakes me away.

"One minute, Skylar. I need to write a comment on this very problematic video about climate change and—" She finally looks up. "It's you," Dana squeaks. "Lilac Eyes. I can't believe it's really you."

Lilac Eyes? Bingo! I knew I recognized them.

Dana then does something super weird: she starts to pat their faces one by one. "Are you holograms?" she asks.

One of the girls, who is wearing a pair of pink cat

ears, tries to duck away from Dana's hands. I don't blame her because a stranger touching your face is weird, plus Dana has unusually clammy hands.

"We're real," she says.

Dana gulps. "Whoa."

"Hi, I'm Mi-Cha. We're heading back to the airport soon, but we found this on the ground outside. It's such a shame to think a fan lost it." She holds up my AZ8 photobook and I gasp so deeply it makes me light-headed.

"It's – it's mine," I stammer. I reach forward to take the photobook and I swear having it back in my arms feels as delightful as someone filling my arms with cash, doughnuts or a tiny-footed baby K-pop idol in a tartan baby grow.

"I'm super impressed with your collection," Mi-Cha says. "You have photocards I have been trying to get hold of for years."

"You like AZ8?" I ask, surprised.

She pulls at the keyring hanging from her jeans. "Yeah. Me and Seri are Glows." She points to the girl in the pink bandana who I guess must be Seri because she bows at me and steps forward.

"AZ8 are the reason we got into K-pop in the first place," Seri explains. "Though Hana and Ha-Yoon are not Glows. They're Flossies." She indicates to the other two band members who have walked over to the Future Stage, where the big lights are off and the digital screen is now dark. Everything is empty apart from a man sweeping up all the leftover sand from Tut's performance.

"How can you be in a band together when you don't even like the same thing?" I ask.

The girls laugh.

"Easy," Mi-Cha says. "It's great to like different things. It's what makes us unique. Us Glows are influenced by soulful pop songs you can dance *and* cry to, whereas the Flossies are influenced by funky dance beats you can play as the soundtrack to your summer barbecue while thinking about the meaning of life."

"Of course." I look at Dana, who grins at this turn of events.

"They're like us," I say. "Different, but…"

"…ultimately the same," she fills in.

We give each other a hug and watch as the girls head over to the stage to join their other two band members. They talk to each other in Korean and at one point giggle at something though judging by their sloped shoulders and slow movements they're not 100 per cent happy.

"Today was meant to be their first ever live performance in Europe," Dana says. "I watched them on *Live-Right-Now* where they talked about rehearsing for up to fifteen hours a day."

"It's so sad they don't get to perform," I say. "Especially as they came all this way."

One of the girls climbs up onto the stage and pretends to hold a mic. She does a little boogie to make the others laugh. Mi-Cha climbs up next and also mimics holding a mic then starts singing in Korean.

"She has a great voice," I say.

"She's super talented," Dana gushes. "They all are. I feel so bad for them."

The other two girls climb up and together they sing a capella. I must admit, it's pretty impressive. Dana and I walk towards the stage, and I take advantage of the speedy Wi-Fi to stream their song on my phone.

They begin to sing along, *"Water runs through your fingers, ooh I make it linger."* Then they do the dance routine, which involves a lot of swinging around, cowgirl style, combined with fluid wave-like movements of the hips.

Whoa, girl group dancing is so different from the stompy, energic routines typical of AZ8. I'm not saying one is better than the other, because I think I like both.

"They're so good," I say to Dana.

"I told you," she says, her smile bright. She steps forward and puts her hands out wide. "This is the bit you can join in with … if you want?"

I observe one round of the chorus as the girls and Dana both spin and get their hands to glide around, as if they're streams, then I copy.

Even the cleaner joins in: he swings his broom like a majorette then, in a complete disregard for health and safety, tosses it high in the air. It rotates twice before falling back down, straight into his waiting hands.

"Waaaaa!" the girls scream as he takes a bow and goes back to sweeping up sand.

Lilac Eyes finish with the line, "*Water runs all through the show, it knows where it's got to go, never try to stop the flow.*" They strike a pose and take a bow.

Dana and I clap wildly.

"That was spectacular," Dana says excitedly. "Whoa, I'm so glad I got to see it."

The girls help each other down from the stage. "And we're so glad we got to perform for someone."

"*Gamsahamida,*" Hana says. "Thank you for being an awesome audience."

Their manager comes over to call them back to their tour bus, and they each bow at us before waving goodbye.

Dana's face is all red and blotchy, in a good way. "I can't believe what just happened."

"I know, that was so cool."

I flinch when my phone rings, the unmistakable sound of AZ8's "Snow Falls Around the Tree", which despite being a Christmas song is perfect for all seasons.

"Hi, Nana," I say into my phone.

"What are you girls doing in there for so long? We need to get home. I need to put the whatsit in the microwave and the doodah in the pressure cooker."

"We're coming, Nana, we just stopped to—"

She tuts. "You must think I have all the time in the world to stand around waiting for you. Hurry up."

As I hang up I can't help but laugh, because if you ask me, time is one thing Nana has too much of.

20

ONE WEEK LATER

Dana sits on the sofa next to me and pats the spot between us. But Kookie isn't having it.

"Why won't she sit with us anymore?" Dana moans.

"Because she's an absolute diva."

At this comment, Kookie flicks her tail in the air, pads in a little circle and makes herself comfortable on her new special *throne* over by the window. Nana said she found the cat throne on a website called cutpricecatstuff. com, but when I looked it up, no such website exists. There's also something about the gold and blue colour scheme which rings a little familiar. As does most of the stuff Nana brings back from her "travels".

The front door opens, and seconds later slams shut.

"Hey, Dad," I call as he walks into the living room in his bright red tracksuit. He pauses, then slowly flops down onto his belly by our feet.

"How was training?" I ask.

"I am never going to run again," he grumbles into the carpet. "My Achilles are screaming at me."

"Really?" I giggle. "What are they saying?"

"*We hate you*," Dad says in a silly squeaky voice.

Dad still spends most of his free time training, but at least he and Mum have worked out a schedule which means I'm not left alone all weekend ever again. I've also thought long and hard about things and concluded that Shakespeare was right. Not about *A Midsummer Night's Dream* – that still makes no sense – but about change being something I shouldn't fear.

Dana and I continue our work, tapping away on our laptops at the extra History assignment we were given after claiming Henry VIII had six wives, because apparently, he had five, and no one has ever heard of Catherine Howard.

Nana comes in from the kitchen, carrying a pile of burritos. "Now let's see, I have the Curie curried orange and paneer for Dana."

Dana reaches over to grab it. "Yum. *Merci!*"

"Protein-packed Tut-toasted tuna for you, my little running man." At this, Dad lifts a weak hand to grab his paper-wrapped burrito.

"Shakespearean whole chicken for Skylar. And for

me, the Just-how-your-mama-used-to-make-it-special. Although, the spinach stew in this was made by…"

"Yours truly," I say proudly. I unwrap my own burrito quicker than you can say *To be, or not to be,* and tuck in. "Mmm, this is the very best."

"No way," Dana chimes in, her mouth full. "If there was a Nobel Prize for best tortilla-based snack, *this* would win it." Her watch beeps. "Ooh, it's almost time."

Dad rolls over onto his back and yawns. "Remind me what this is again?"

"It's the worldwide premiere of the new Lilac Eyes video," I say.

"Lilac Eyes?" Nana questions. "Those singing boys in the skinny trousers you like?"

"No, Nana. Lilac Eyes is a girl group."

"I thought you hated girl groups," Dad says.

I roll my eyes at him. "I changed my mind. Because change is good for your cognitive health, right, Dana?"

Dana smiles and nods.

"Also," I say in between bites, "there's an Internet rumour about the song having a special guest feature from a boy band. So, you know what this means?"

"That there's going to be way too many people singing on one song?" Dad says as he takes a bite and chews with great effort.

We ignore him, though it's true. I am also concerned about how you divide up song lyrics between twelve people. Guess I'll find out soon enough.

The screen goes to black, and in yellow the words "Sands of Time" come up, causing Dana and I to wiggle our eyebrows excitedly at each other.

Then Woojin, the lead singer of AZ8, appears on the screen.

HANA

Role: Lead singer

Biggest fear: The dark

Fun fact: Used to be an opera singer before pursuing K-pop

MI-CHA

Role: Leader

Special skills:
Can speak six languages, including Klingon

Signature look: Her Cruella de Vil hair

Fun fact: Mi-Cha has the world's largest collection of AZ8 photocards

LILAC EYES FACT FILES

SERI

Role: Maknae
(baby of the group)

Favourite things:
Kittens, cartoons and
unicorns

Fun fact: Her cousin is
AZ8 superstar Woojin

HA-YOON

Role: Lead dancer

Special skill: Achieved a PhD in Astrophysics
alongside recording Lilac Eyes' debut album

Fun fact: Can eat six tofu wraps
in under an hour

QUIZ:
Which historical idol are you?

How would you describe your style?

a) All black everything

b) F-A-B-U-L-O-U-S!

c) Bling, bling

What's your party trick?

a) You don't need tricks when your mind is
   this brilliant

b) Making theatre audiences weep with
   my brilliance

c) Singing while sandboarding

What are you most likely to say?

a) Thank you for this Nobel Prize

b) To be, or not to be, that is the question

c) You make sand witch

Mostly As: You're as impressive as double Nobel Prize-winning Marie Curie.
Mostly Bs: You're as fabulous as the bard of London, William Shakespeare.
Mostly Cs: You're as bling as the boy king, Tut.

What's your favourite meal?

a) Who has time to eat when there are discoveries to be made?

b) Periwinkles with a dash of hot pepper sauce

c) Feta cheeeese!

Favourite emoji?

a) 🧠 Brain

b) 🎭 Theatre faces/masks

c) 🥪 Sandwich

How would your friends describe you?

a) Brilliant, inspirational, fantastical

b) A bottomless cavern of literary delights

c) I don't have friend; I have slave

What do you always have in your pocket?

a) Citrus fruit

b) Small paintings of my handsome face to give to adoring fans

c) Sand

ACKNOWLEDGEMENTS

I could write a thousand **SONNETS** about my gratitude towards my amazing agent Eve White and fellow **BARDS** Ludo Cinelli and Steven Evans.

Thank you, fellow **GLOW** Megan Middleton, for making this happen. I love the way you love AZ8 so much, you even went on a break when they did. Thank you, Karen Ball for stepping on stage mid-performance, welcome to the **FANDOM**. And thank you, Jamie Hammond, you are a king in any **ERA**.

Shout out to the entire team at Walker Books, thank you so much for making such great **BURRITOS** … I mean, books. There are Nobel Prizes in the post for all of you. Speaking of burritos, merci to copy editor Jenny Sykes, may your feta always be **CHEESY**.

Thank you, Amy Nguyen, for another **AMAZING** cover and illustrations of Lilac Eyes, I'd drag a photobook of your work to the **ENDS OF TIME**.

The biggest bowl of spinach stew to Emmanuella Dekonor, for helping to make Nana's Ghanaian home *home* home **POP**.

Finally, thanks to Annabelle, you'll always be a **CUTIE PATOOTIE** to me, and to Patrick, who I would marry six times over and never have **BEHEADED**.

About the Author

LUAN GOLDIE is a writer of children's books as well as short stories and novels for adults. She worked in primary schools for over a decade where she loved teaching PE and anything which involved clay, paint or glitter.

When not writing, Luan can be found teaching writing to others, hanging upside down at a fitness class, or watching K-pop music videos. Her ult bias is Kim Namjoon from BTS.